EAST A
the GEM

This compendium portrays a wonderful way of life
lived in the 1950s and 60s in East Africa.

J Trotter

WINGSPUR PUBLICATIONS

East Africa the Gem
© **J Trotter** 2015

Published by
WINGSPUR PUBLICATIONS
wingspur@virginmedia.com

ISBN 978-0-9931304-0-3

Printed by Blissetts Bookbinders
Roslin Road, Acton, London W3 8DH

To Cynthia and Julia

Foreword

The delights of life in East Africa during its colonial period are well described in a multitude of memoirs by many who were privileged to live in such a uniquely challenging, stimulating and fascinating environment. Few other countries had such a diversity of climate, topography, wild life, and personal opportunities to be enjoyed by those who pioneered its early development.

Whilst many memoirs reflect years of mature judgement, Jimmy Trotter now presents a tale of youthful adventure which differs both in style and context. The immediate post-war years were days when young newly arrived bachelors either lived or perished in their enthusiastic hair-raising adventures. Jimmy was one of those who survived. He now presents a compendium of well written and amusing anecdotes which could only have happened to a young 'pioneer' in the private sector who had neither bureaucratic, political nor even social axes to grind. His ability to blend into the local scene and to seek out similarly minded extroverts (for which East Africa was famous) gives added spice to his tale.

Jimmy's adventures, particularly those relating to the realities of unescorted hunting, make enthralling reading. His accounts portray the initiative taken by an enthusiastic and nervous young man who had absolutely no experience in the rigours, realities and dangers of 'big game hunting'. With only a bare minimum of equipment, little professional advice and lots of courage, his sorties, with big game were remarkably successful: his vivid accounts illustrate an adventurous spirit and a strong character.

This lively presentation of stories covers the broad spectrum of 20 years spent in East Africa, including marriage to his delightful wife Cynthia. During this time he travelled extensively in all three countries as he progressed up the ladder of company promotion; in itself, this provides an entry into a world seldom covered by others, which makes his comments all the more fascinating. His unforeseen departure from East Africa, following disturbing political mayhem in Uganda, serves as a poignant reminder of how events can, so easily, destroy our dreams.

It is my pleasure to introduce Jimmy's adventures. We both arrived in East Africa as enthusiastic bachelors, at much the same time. And although our paths never crossed, my own life was also dominated by an equally close involvement with the natural environment in many of the areas which he describes. I am pleased to vouch for the accuracy of detail and to confirm the reality of the situations which he portrays. We have been close friends for a number of years through our mutual interest in our joint experiences – I never cease to be enthralled by his gift as a raconteur.

Kenneth Sargent OBE BSc
Ex Forest Officer, Kenya

Acknowledgements

I have received an enormous amount of encouragement from Cynthia, Ken and Joan. Cynthia has braved my longhand scrawl and typed the whole manuscript – twice! My very good friends Ken and Joan have proof-read the script and given me enthusiastic inspiration without which I would not have completed the book. Joan's knowledge of the written word is awesome.

Thank you Graham (maps), John (cover graphics) and Michael (cover photograph)

My right-hand stalwart, advisor, computer-wizard and un-complaining friend Kelvin has helped me through thick and thin.
I am grateful to you all.

JT

Contents

Illustrations

1

Introduction

You will die of Black Water Fever.

Doesn't malaria kill?

Where on earth is Dar es Salaam?

What's the matter with Cape Town?

Dar es what?

These were some of the comforting overtures emanating from a number of my learned friends when I announced that I was leaving for Dar es Salaam, early in l95l.

After completing my schooling I spent two and a half years training to be a Chartered Accountant in the 'Mother City' of South Africa. I had almost reached half-way through my articles but needed a further two and a half years to write more exams and qualify.

Cape Town is a beautiful city and I enjoyed those two and a half years except for one snag. I loathed the weather. Snow sometimes fell more than half-way down Table Mountain reaching near to the outskirts of the city in the winter. It was cold. When it was not snowing it was raining – freezing winter rain. There is no other wind like that of Cape Town, where it blows three hundred and sixty four days a year.

I read an accounting journal which came to our office monthly in which the position of Audit Clerk was being advertised as vacant in Dar es Salaam. The advertiser was Gill and Johnson of Nairobi and the successful applicant would take up his appointment in their branch in Dar es Salaam. A three-year contract with two and a half months' paid leave to South Africa sounded like a heaven-sent opportunity to me.

I applied. An interview was arranged and a dignitary from Deloitte, Plender, Griffiths, Annan & Co (Accountants) telephoned and I was summoned to their plush offices. One of their partners interviewed (grilled) me for forty-five minutes. Finally, (words were few in those days), he said "Hmff, I will write and tell them what I think of you" and dismissed me from his presence. I scuttled out of his illustrious preserve as speedily and silently as possible.

Washing the whole episode from my mind I returned to work and forgot all about it. Two weeks later, a letter arrived from Gill and Johnson offering me the position. Would I accept the conditions outlined in the rest of the epistle?

East Africa, near the equator, hot and exotic-sounding to my ears, wide open spaces, alive with big game. Accept them I did and this was the beginning of my move to East Africa.

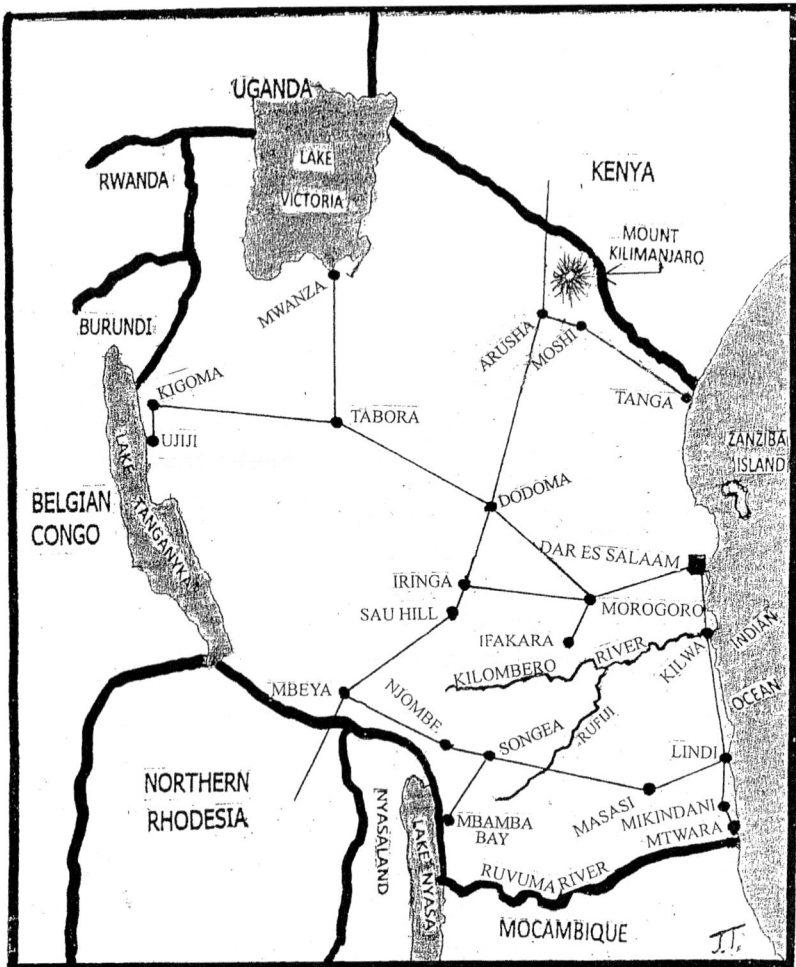

TANGANYIKA

2

Tanganyika

1951

Gill & Johnson flew me from Cape Town to Dar es Salaam. It took three days by Dakota number VP KHN. First stop Durban and then night-stop at the tiny village of Mocambique – half way between Lourenço Marques (Maputo) and Dar es Salaam. A picturesque little place in colonial Portuguese times. Very hot in April 1951. I used the fan all night in the small *banda* which was my room, palm leaves roof, no ceiling and my first introduction to a mosquito net.

I proceeded to the bar before dinner, ordered a beer and was given a 'dinner plate size' platter of King Prawns to go with it. This was a start that suited me down to the 'palate'

We landed at Dar es Salaam the following day, mid-day, at Kurasini 'airport' which consisted of a landing strip with two palm leaf shacks as airport buildings. Jim Storey, Manager of Gill & Johnson met me and we proceeded to the New Africa Hotel. What bliss! A big white old Colonial building; square, with courtyard in the centre and walls two feet thick. No air-conditioning but electric fans hung from every ceiling. The smell of disinfectant and stale booze predominated. Laundry handed in at five p.m. and returned two hours later all clean, dry and ironed. The staff wore long white robes with no pockets and a red fez. A three-piece band - piano, violin and drums - twanged out a series of old-fashioned tunes from six till eight p.m. and at lunch times. A very active bar was situated on the courtyard. I was not prepared for the humidity and heat although I had been forewarned. Fortunately the clothing we wore in the day time was suited to the weather; white stockings, white shorts and white open-necked shirt with short sleeves. This was the official dress for all office workers in colonial Dar es Salaam.

Dar es Salaam harbour with palm trees, ships-in-harbour, *ngalawas* (canoes with two outriggers and sail) and *dhows,* was a magical place. A heavy tropical perfume pervaded the whole harbour area which was overtaken every now and then by the scent of spices which the Indian merchants imported or shipped.

Such was Dar es Salaam. I happily soaked up this atmosphere and plunged into the marvellous life-style existing at that

Ship leaving harbour, Dar es Salaam

Heaven of Peace Harbour

time. Gill & Johnson's office in Acacia Avenue was the usual dusty & dull accountant-type establishment but the staff were very amicable and went out of their way to make things pleasant for the new arrival. Our building was the only one in Acacia Avenue with a lift which was visible from the kerbside. It had iron grill gates so one could see the lift going up and down. As a result we normally had an audience of the *indigini* standing and gazing at this great *wazungu* (white-man's) carrying machine. These were usually bush dwellers who had come into town for supplies and this was one of the sights not to be missed.

The local African was incredibly primitive, very friendly and at the same time, a charming person who was keen to teach and encourage Swahili to any newcomer. I learned as quickly as I could and my ability to speak Zulu was an advantage as both are Bantu languages, although Swahili has a substantial proportion of Arabic in it.

Well, back to the *New Africa Hotel* - my company paid for a few weeks until I found digs. It was extremely pleasant. Whisky was threepence a tot and the cheapest drink to buy, what a pleasure! Fortunately, my Pa had advised me not to drink during the day. "Never start until sundown". I stuck to this rule for the rest of my life. However, with whisky at that price I became friendly with a young crowd and at times monumental hangovers were the result.

My first transport was a second-hand Matchless motor cycle 350, all I could afford on the hire purchase finance supplied by my company. I might mention at this stage, that I arrived in Dar es Salaam with the princely sum of fifty pounds as my sole wealth! That did not last very long and I was soon waiting for my first salary.

From the *New Africa* into the Company bachelors' mess, a pleasant abode in Oyster Bay close to the beach with many *baobabs* close by and even one in the garden. My co-tenants were John Lambert and Freddy Clark.

The Dar es Salaam climate is absolutely ideal for motor cyclists and I was able to explore the area at a very low cost; the beaches, the coves, the coral and the spear-fishing in warm balmy water and the proximity of big game. This made our Dar es Salaam especially interesting. The name Dar es Salaam, meant, according to the Swahili gurus 'Haven of Peace' or 'Fragrant Harbour' for reasons I mentioned earlier, but the great **Rufiji** who would have known better than anyone else claimed it meant 'Safe Harbour'. To me Fragrant Harbour sounded more exotic.

Rufiji was one of the more colourful and eccentric characters of Tanganyika. Well-educated at public school in England, he wrote weekly articles in the Tanganyika Standard and these articles were so interesting that all looked forward to reading them. He also published a book - *Rufiji* - which is still in my possession today.

Let us dwell on Rufiji for a while. In 1951 he was an elderly man who had, years before, gone completely *bush* (rejected civilization); one did not know his proper name. The Colonial Government did and he was an embarrassment to them as he was previously a D.O. (District Officer) in the Territory.

Apart from having gone *bush* and not keeping up the 'stiff-upper-lip' upright English gentleman image which the hierarchy in the Tanganyika Government expected of any decent and well-educated Englishman, he continually sniped at the District Commissioners, District Officers and all Government personnel with the most comic and pleasant ridicule in all of his articles. It was fun for all to read.

His knowledge of the bush, the animals and the territory of Tanganyika was phenomenal. He lived on the coast near the Rufiji river mouth, south of Dar es Salaam. He did not know how many wives he had or children but there were many. His wives were of course, African.

He would proceed to Dar es Salaam every two months and his method of travel was on foot with a retinue of bearers. He wore a pith helmet (topee)! After stocking up with supplies and handing over his writings to the editor of the *Tanganyika Standard*, he would spend a night or two in Dar es Salaam and would have a few noggins at the *Metropole* or the *New Africa Hotel* and then proceed with his twenty to thirty bearers, with loads on heads, all in line and him at the head of the column, back to his beloved bush life. He was an accomplished hunter and an acknowledged expert on the flora and fauna of Tanganyika.

In later years, after I was married, I was to discover that my wife had worked in a government office (railways) with one of Rufiji's daughters. She worked in the same office as Cynthia where she was a most efficient stenographer with a very pleasant personality and was married to an English gentleman.

Now, back to my part. Our bachelors' Mess at Oyster Bay was, for the most part, reasonably well run. We took it in weekly turns to manage the running with the help one *mpishi* (cook), one houseboy and a *shamba* (garden) boy. We lived pretty well and all three of us had jobs which took us on safari all over Tanganyika.

I was very fortunate to travel to almost every corner of Tanganyika during the first two years. All travel was by air. The places where I worked (as an audit clerk) were Iringa, Mbeya, Lindi, Tabora, Mufindi (tea company), Uruwira Minerals at Mpanda and Mtwara.

On safari we worked in pairs and I had either Freddy Clark or a Mr Wright with me. I was always the junior one. Our general routine was to work the day through, then shower and make for the bar – drink until five minutes before the dining-room was due to be closed, rush in and then noisily demand to go through the whole menu. Most times I would just make it, with perhaps some others from the bar; but Freddy would frequently not make it and then push his way through the closed doors, stagger past the stony-faced waiters, announce to the whole dining room audience that the hotel clocks were wrong and that he would now partake of his meal. Normally he would get away with it but on some occasions he would not and then he would turn round and wind a zigzag path through the tables and nose his way through a haze of alcohol back to the bar.

He was never late for work in the mornings but nine times out of ten would still have sufficient whisky flowing through his veins to be quite merry at the start of the day and then start dozing towards midday, sleep a siesta straight after lunch, push through the afternoon as fast as possible and proceed through the whole routine all over again.

When I was paired with old Pop Wright it was an entirely different story. He must have been in his seventies, would drink tea throughout the day, sweat gallons of perspiration, change his shirt three times a day, smoke one cigarette after another in a long cigarette holder and tell me - if pressed hard enough - of the good times he had had forty years earlier on the Lupa goldfields rush in southern Tanganyika near Chunya. He was an old-timer and yes, still wore a topee. A thorough gentleman.

On one occasion Pop Wright and I were sent to Mkoe Sisal Estate near Lindi to do an audit. We flew to Lindi and an African gentleman was our driver who met us at the air-strip to take us to Mkoe Sisal Estate, a distance of probably fifty miles over some atrocious roads in very hilly terrain. The vehicle was a short-wheelbased Land Rover. In those days (195I-2) all vehicles which were any distance from Dar es Salaam were poorly supplied with spare parts and vehicle services were a very rare phenomenon. Ninety percent of the vehicles in Lindi were Land Rovers and ninety per cent of those were so tatty as to be seen to be believed.

Pop recognized our transport and driver, I don't know how, and in we jumped. No good. Get out again and push start. A blue cloud of smoke poured from the back and enveloped us as Hamisi, (our pilot), accelerated and shot forward twenty yards. He reversed with a big smile and we hopped in. I was in the middle and Pop was on my left. What an astonishing vehicle. No shock-absorbers, brakes only just operational, chassis seemed bent, broken spring on front left, power – only just - steering-wheel seemed to travel miles round before the front wheels responded. Our Hamisi seemed not to notice this and drove with great gusto chatting to Pop in Swahili, which I had not yet been able to grasp, and smiled, laughed and swept along. Old Pop had a look of quiet terror on his face and stared straight ahead answering reluctantly in monosyllables. Only rarely did Hamisi seem to look for any length of time at the road ahead so intent was he on chatting to Pop.

We came down a hill, crossed a narrow bridge at speed, shot up the other side but it wasn't steep enough to slow us down much when the road curved sharply right. Hamisi almost lost control but managed to broadside the vehicle round the bend with a high cliff on our right and a sheer drop on our left. Old Pop had the view, I didn't, being in the middle, and he just peered out over the side of the Land Rover into a deep abyss whilst broad-siding. He pulled his head in, leaned back in his seat and wailed "God save us" as we straightened up. Hamisi smiled his way onwards. Pop's prayer was answered – we arrived in one piece.

The Land Rovers of that time, especially the short wheelbase model, gave one's shoulder blades a continual banging by the back-rest if the shock-absorbers were a bit worn. Those in Hamisi's Land Rover were pretty-well non-existent so, due to his age, old Pop arrived a trifle back sore, but in good spirits to have arrived at all. I was terrified most of the journey.

When checking labour attendance cards (kipandes), Pop would frequently read the comments on the rear of these cards which had been in the possession of the labourers and had become very grubby due to frequent handling. Things like "did not arrive until nine a.m. on Monday" or "found sleeping on duty" or "came to work drunk" or "dismissed for stealing"; when once he held up a card gingerly between two fingers and looked down his nose through his pince-nez with infinite distaste at the note on the back which read "died of smallpox". He went off in a hurry to the bathroom and washed his hands.

Tanganyika was colonial at that period but independence *(Uhuru)* was frequently mentioned amongst the rumblings and grumblings of the emerging politicians. The name Julius Nyerere had appeared on the political stage. We were told at Mkoe that the General Manager had been fired two weeks earlier because the name of his dog, which was printed on the collar, was Julius! That was 1953. He was put on a plane and deported back to Holland.

Back to life in Dar es Salaam. I moved from our Oyster Bay mess to one in town run by Yvon Savy whom I had already met. He and one Scot, (can't remember name) wanted someone to share expenses to reduce the cost of living. I was therefore closer to work and the Gymkhana Club which was a convenient waterhole and where, oh yes, we played tennis as well. A fine club with plenty of activity, mainly tennis. Plenty of lovely people. The best girls in Dar es Salaam went there and the men's bar was a place of roaring activity every night. There was golf, tennis, rugby and hockey and frequent *do's* like dances, celebrations etc. etc. All in all, a very active meeting place for all the young sportsmen and women and drinkers of Dar es Salaam. As the difference between the hot season and the cool season made very little difference to the sport (except rugger and hockey), all sorts of tournaments were always on the go.

Spear fishing on coral reefs

It was after about six months that I started spear fishing. The Dar coast and numerous islands were bordered by the most magnificent coral reefs and consequently the marine-life matched the magnificence of the coral. Snorkel, goggles, spear gun, flippers, a floating knife, string round the waist for securing the catch; - that was all the equipment needed. We would hire an *ngalawa* (locally built outrigger canoe) if we wanted to go to one of the islands for a day. The sea could be quite treacherous and we did on a few occasions have a hectic crossing but the skippers were very good and frequently had us baling at great speed if things became very rough. The *ngalawa* had no motor – just a sail - and went very well. Normally the weather was good and the sea was always lovely and warm. One would look for rock-cod, parrot fish or the shoals of game-fish (barracuda, queen fish, kole-kole etc) for the pot and we always came back with large catches of these species which, in later years, when each of us had married, our wives would fry, poach, bake, pickle, smoke, boil or curry. We would never return without crayfish which were most plentiful and large – we never took any under half a kilo (one pound) and the largest I brought home weighed in at about five pounds (two and a half kilos). We grew tired of eating fish and shell-fish.

I joined the Yacht Club and crewed for some of the skippers during weekend races and on a number of occasions, a few of us would get together and go out to Honeymoon Island for a picnic. It was a marvellous place with lovely beaches, some dense bush, a wide, flat reef of coral and tepid water in which to swim. Naturally we spear fished (goggled).

It is not for me to describe the variety of colourful marine life in the East African waters as this has been more professionally done in many books on the subject but suffice it to say that I found a new world in those tropical waters and coral reefs. During many goggling trips with Yvon Save, Andy Knott, René Vidot, Brian O'Toole, Gerry Pershouse, Alec Varcoe, David Etock, John Pepperell and others whose names I forget, I had some very exciting experiences. We all did.

It was generally expected that sharks would be encountered when the water was murky. Andy and I formed a pattern which gave us moral comfort and some sort of defence when danger appeared. We would always go out as a pair and keep within sight and hailing distance of each other. When sharks or a big shoal of barracuda appeared we would get close to each other, back to back, and in turns face the shark which normally circled around us, until it moved off. The barracuda would come straight at us and stop one or two yards away, (sometimes closer) – peer at us with mouths opening very widely and then closing in a sort of belligerent chewing action which seemed as though they were intent on having us for lunch. I heard of some bad attacks by barracuda but never spoke to anyone who had gone through the experience.

On one occasion I was goggling in shallow water approximately six feet deep on a coral bank in murky water. I was gliding along the surface, some distance from the shore, as we had come out by boat. Intent on peering at the nooks and crannies for crayfish I therefore looked straight down as I cruised along the reef-edge. I could hardly believe my eyes when I realized that I was suddenly peering, not at the coral any more, but at a grey mass of shark sliding underneath me. It was huge – the girth seemed to be about two-and-a-half feet across at the widest point of the torso. I had no time to take any evasive action at all, not that that would have been in any way effective. I could have stretched my hand down and touched it. No intention of doing that though, thank you. The sheer mass and the effortless ease as it passed beneath me made me realize what little chance one would have against a powerful killer of that sort if it decided that lunch-time had come. I poked my head up and alarmed the other gogglers who were some way off. Fortunately none of them had a visit from my monster friend.

On another occasion Andy Knott and I were out in a boat belonging to Yvon Save and anchored near Honeymoon Island. The water was, as usual, crystal clear. Four of us were goggling. Sting-rays were frequently found in our waters and were a tempting challenge with a spear gun. Catches of one hundred and fifty pounds and more had been boasted by some gogglers and the task of bringing them in was great fishing sport as the larger ones frequently defeated the spear -fisherman.

When a sting-ray spotted a fisherman coming, and he spotted you long before you spotted him, it would always flatten itself on the sea-bed and wriggle and wriggle until the sand covered it all over except for the two eyes and the wing tips. One would therefore always look for this silhouette when swimming over sandy areas. When spotted, a ray would streak off if it was approached roughly and without care. If one approached carefully without splashing or wriggling too much whilst diving, one could quite often get a shot into the heavy flesh close to and outside the eyes – (bone lies between the eyes) and the spear barb would get a good solid grip. Any shot further out towards the end of the wings would ensure the ray's escape.

I spotted a good sized silhouette. It seemed pretty large so I eased out of alarm-range and called Andy to come and cover me when I made first shot. If I missed then he could have a go at the moving target. I dived, fired the harpoon and it entered the correct area. Within a split second, Andy had plunged his harpoon into the heavy flesh on the other side of the eyes. These were two solid shots into it and it took off at high speed with both of us being pulled through the water. I must say I was surprised at its strength. The size was larger than I had expected and the distance from where it took off and the spot to where it suddenly sounded at the end of the run

Author holding shark

27

must have been not less than thirty to forty yards. It settled in the sand and then took off again and headed, fortunately for us, into shallower water. This time the run was not quite so fierce. However, it took us another fifteen to twenty minutes to subdue in water approximately ten feet deep. It plunged, turned, jumped and by the time it was sufficiently tired to start pulling towards the boat, the water was churned up into a brown colour. Handling this heavyweight into the boat was another matter and it is surprising how heavy it was to lift from a swimming position (two men in the water and one in the boat) into the boat. I recall that the weight was about one hundred and thirty pounds.

A shipwreck, sardines, shark and octopus

The wreck of the *Slemmestad* lay about two miles from the mouth of Dar es Salaam harbour. The deepwater channel for vessels from the harbour-mouth out to sea took a winding path and it was comparatively narrow so that ships had to navigate accurately along the middle of the channel where the depth was good enough for all normal passenger ships and cargo vessels. But the channel sides were steep coral and shaped up to a plateau of coral . Ships normally entered and left Dar es Salaam harbour at high tides but even so it was necessary to keep to the beaten track, as the skipper, or harbour pilot must have found out when the *Slemmestad* ran aground on the coral edge of the channel. I have no doubt that the skipper or harbour pilot never knew what a gift he was presenting to the spear-fisherman of Dar es Salaam. I often marvelled at what a great sport he was.

The ship lay on coral which, at high-tide, was difficult to fish but at neap tides we could fish high or low tide. It was a large cargo ship and must have been on the sea-bed for about ten years and in an upright position. The deck had collapsed along a large area amidships, and the outer skin of the port side of the ship seemed to have vanished so that where the deck collapsed, the steel bunkers underneath were squashed down and as a result, layer upon layer of buckled steel was visible to the goggler and was the home of a myriad of fish. These layers were dark and inaccessible but the residences of a never-ending supply of rock-cod. The layers in most places were only about two feet apart at the outer-most point and tapered inwards in a wedge shape and all covered in seaweed which waved back and forth with the currents. The cod therefore had a convenient place into which they could retreat safe from the harpoon, but close to a never-ending stream of small fish which travelled past and which provided nosh unlimited.

However, a rock-cod is a curious beast and would often peer out at the goggler swimming past. Mouthing at the fisherman it would present a reasonable target. The harpoon would best be aimed at the mouth or gills. The cod would then invariably reverse or turn into its cave and spread its lateral fins out to get a firm grip on the sides of its abode. If the spearfisher pulled too hard the harpoon would come out and the fish be lost and it was therefore difficult to judge how much one should tug. Most times this all happened at a depth which was beyond the length of the cord from harpoon to gun and so one was obliged to fire, have a good tug, and then with shortage of air, decide whether to leave gun dangling upwards (it floated) and swim to the surface, or stay down with lungs bursting and have a go at either tugging harder or pushing the harpoon further in by hand to get complete penetration from one side of the fish to the other and consequently have more chance of a successful retrieve. One would always have the fear that if the gun was left whilst going up for air that it would have disappeared by the time the fisherman had taken in air and gone down again. It was not unknown for some unsporting fish to scarper with a harpoon gun. The *Slemmestad* was a good home and a good hunting ground.

René Vidot was the most successful spear fisherman and all-round fisherman I had the privilege of fishing with for many years. He, Yvon Save, Andy Knott and myself proceeded one Sunday in Save's boat to the *Slemmestad*. It was not quite the right time of the tide (too deep) and so we cruised further north towards a well-known island (name forgotten) but as we left the *Slemmestad* we noticed birds diving into the water. It is always wise to investigate this sort of commotion and when we got closer, our interest grew as we saw the water boiling with fish, small ones, which the gulls were swooping down and feeding upon. Of further significance was the fact that we could see, in this clear water, larger fish circling around the shoal of sardines. This jamboree was taking place over the deep water of the channel for the ships.

Yvon approached at a very slow pace so as not to disturb the shoal. We stopped in the middle; sardines all round us, gulls swooping and taking mouthfuls of these small fish which were about three inches in length. I would estimate that the surface area of the sardines was in the region of twenty-five yards across and beyond that were the big fish. It was easy to spot the shark fins which had joined the game-fish and all were making forays into the sardines. We donned goggles and hung our torsos over the boat gunwale into the water.

It was crystal clear and very deep. An extraordinary sight met our eyes; the game-fish, kole-kole and queen fish mainly, together with a number of various sharks of all sizes, were coming in and taking great mouthfuls of sardines. They were all so close that we grabbed our harpoon guns and landed three or four kole-kole in quick succession. This was done without getting our feet wet. We simply hung over the boat and with goggles on and shoulders and chest in the water, fired away. The reason for our non-entry into the water was the size of some of the sharks. No thanks – there was a hammerhead of about nine feet in length and other big, nasty-looking brutes which seemed to take in gallons of sardines as they came in.

After landing about four kole-kole (cannot remember exactly how many as this was a wild picnic) they became wary of the boat and would not come within range. René suddenly took a decision. He theorized that the sharks which were enjoying such a good meal on the sardines, and with hardly any effort, would not be interested in eating the likes of us. I was sceptical and Yvon and Andy seemed suddenly reluctant to enter into the water. René mocked us for our timidity but Yvon assured him that after he had tested his theory and was not eaten, he, Yvon would join René to give him some company.

Without further ado René slipped into the water quietly and with us watching proceeded to harpoon two lovely kole-kole. The sharks were uninterested and circled and came in normally and took more mouthfuls of sardines. We three then slipped into the water as well. It was an eerie experience. The big hammerhead was a particularly savage-looking creature but paid scant attention to us. The other sharks seemed to mind their manners as well and so we brought in a number of the game fish. We must have been in the water for about ten minutes. Two of us were still in the water and two in the boat and I was remaining close to the shoal waiting for any incoming fish. I kept abreast of the main concentration of sardines and kept an eye on the sharks which seemed to accept us as fellow partakers of the feast. Andy nudged me and I surfaced to hear what he wanted. He suggested that the fish were becoming wary of us so "let's have a go at a shark".

This was, I suspected, a very risky pastime but I went along with him and we selected a small to medium-sized chap of about fifty pounds. I had the first shot and put the harpoon into its gills at almost point blank range. It was a most telling shot entering very well but the struggle was on and I did not know who was going to win. Andy then came in with a particularly accurate shot under extremely difficult circumstances as it was going berserk on the end of my harpoon and doing all sorts of acrobatics. His shot went in under the dorsal fin and so we had two anchorages to enable us to hold down its struggle. We soon had it into the boat and then carried on swimming but the shoal sounded and we found them to be out of reach. The shark was a mean fish in the boat; he wanted to bite all of us. Our weight estimation was wrong and although it looked like a medium to small size to us in the water, the weight was only forty pounds.

I have mentioned before that René Vidot was good at spear-fishing. He was in fact a more accomplished fisherman in all respects than any other of the many dozens of us who took to the water in search of pleasure and fishing.

Born in the Seychelles, as was Yvon Save, educated there and looking for work after education, he came to Tanganyika. There was not much else to do in the Seychelles except fish and chase the girls, he told me. I don't know why he left. However, leave he did and joined the Tanganyika Government and took up Land Surveying. As this meant that at least half of his working-life he was in the bush, it suited his other passion – hunting. He soon became an accomplished hunter and naturalist. One could rely on his knowledge for almost any answers regarding, not only sea creatures but those in the big and small game categories on land as well.

Let us go back to the sea. René had explained to me on occasions how to neutralize an octopus. Although I had seen many and tried to harpoon a few, I had never tried out his method of turning the body and head inside-out with the hands. To harpoon them was ineffective as they just stuck to the coral with tentacles in all sorts of nooks and crevices. The effect of the harpoon penetrating the head or body seemed not to bother the octopus and it was most puzzling to make out which was head and which was body. In addition to this, the black ink which it would squirt from its main orifice into the water and which obscured its bodywork and head and all round for a distance of about three to four feet, made it a most difficult customer to deal with. A thoroughly unsporting sea creature. Creature yes, but fish no. What is it? I would imagine that a fish is a vertebrate animal. This thing has no vertebrae and no shell that one can feel or see. Just a sort of beak which tapers mostly and which cannot be termed as bone-hard. Eat it? Not likely when it looked so reprehensible.

But no, I was wrong, eating it was a delicacy and René knew all about the niceties of the culinary preparation of octopus. He did in fact know how to prepare and cook just about every creature in the sea but I will come to that later.

He and I were wallowing along near Kunduchi on the reef enjoying ourselves and had taken a couple of fish each. I cannot remember exactly how many but he always had more fish around his waist than I did as he always shot two to my one. With his eagle eyes he spotted a dome in the coral, heavily camouflaged as octopuses always are. No sign of the tentacles but whoever dreamt of one of those heads without those disgusting sucker-ridden, rather slimy, long, tapering tentacles. What a horrible name – tentacle. Anyhow, down went René and after giving me his gun to hold I watched with interest to see him put his words into practice. He gently eased his fingers underneath the dome and then gave a vigorous pull. He had plenty of strength as he was a tall lean man with a fine physique and sinews like piano-wire.

The octopus had been taken by surprise and three quarters of it came up with most tentacles still wrapped around portions of coral or hanging on to crevices. The free tentacles quickly found René's arms and he gave another tug and up it all came. It had, in the meantime, ejected its usual black ink into the water and I was only just able to make out man and octopus grappling with each other. The tentacles had now slithered up his arms and into his armpits and the tips had reached behind his neck although he held it at arms-length. The whole thing was then over in a flash. He had used the thumbs of both hands to press on the head and his fingers to grip the lip at the base of the head near the position where the tentacles are joined to the body/head. There is a round orifice at the base which makes the 'head/body' look like a shallow pocket and he had, with fingers and thumbs, turned this pocket inside-out thus causing the instant death of the octopus.

It was an impressive display of skill by a true Seychellois fisherman. There was never any bravado about this man. He was quietly-spoken and unflappable in that French-accented English and during many spear-fishing and hunting safaris, was one of the finest companions I had in Dar es Salaam.

One day, coming from the town past *Chez Margo* and approaching Salander Bridge on the way to Oyster Bay on my motor-cycle, I spotted a familiar figure standing near the bridge with a small crowd gathered around him - René - and what was he doing there? I stopped and approached and saw what he had captured this time. A sea turtle. He had turned it upside down to prevent its escape. Apparently he had spotted it just beyond Oyster Bay beach in a small sandy cove near the 'Ocean Breeze'. As it was so large and heavy he had sensibly seen the difficulties ahead if he killed it on the spot – it would have been almost impossible to have carried it up the cliffs to Ocean Breeze where there was a road for a vehicle or to drag it over the beaches in Oyster Bay; so he spent a few hours leading it on a cord tied to a front leg, and travelled along the shallow water over the reef for approximately two miles! Ending up at Salander Bridge had enabled him to load it, with plenty of help, into his Ford Pilot station wagon. A week later he invited my fiancée and I to a René and Helen cooked turtle meal. It started off with turtle soup, then on to turtle steaks with all sorts of accompanying delicacies which I cannot remember, until the dessert, which was the only dish not related to the turtle. Helen, his charming wife of Scottish origin had acted on his instructions during cooking, using his Seychellois culinary expertise to produce this exotic but marvellous meal.

René's turtle

Night Fishing at Dar Es Salaam

Captain Jacques Cousteau, the renowned marine explorer, writer, diver, ichthyologist and subsequently TV presenter and radio broadcaster was an incomparable authority on all aspects of the fishes, goggling and diving on the coral reefs of the world. He wrote a comprehensive book on goggling and diving during his early years called *The Silent World* and it became a best seller which most of us read during the fifties. In it he wrote, and I quote from memory:

> "after having experimented by taking to the waters at night-time on a goggling trip in a moment of madness; I would advise my readers never to attempt this form of goggling as it is extremely dangerous and exposes oneself to the perils of deep sea creatures, unseen to the night swimmer. It is foolhardy in the extreme and should never be attempted".

Peter Gorbold in Dar es Salaam must have disagreed, or never read his book. I never discovered which.

So, Peter set himself up with a motor-car tyre inner-tube, twelve volt motor car battery and sealed-beam headlamp. He strapped a couple of wooden planks to one side of the tube which formed the platform for the battery. The sealed beam hand-held lamp was connected with a length of wire flex of comfortable length to the battery and *voilà* the simple set-up was ready for the water. He then tied a towrope to the tube and secured the other end on to his waist-band. He was a robust man with a well-known record of competitive swimming when he was a few years younger in England. He then experimented with this rig during daylight hours and all seemed to function admirably.

Horror of horrors – he invited Andy Knott and myself to accompany him on a maiden nocturnal jamboree. I initially looked for excuses to 'chicken out' but Andy looked at it philosophically and purposely aroused my curiosity instincts which seemed to overpower fears to some extent.

I do not know why, but Peter chose a black night. No moon. This made for even worse foreboding as we carried the equipment down to the water's edge. Peter was his normal effervescent self, bubbling over with the efficiency of his new toy; I just wished he would belt up. Andy was suddenly quiet. It occurred to me loudly and clearly that I must be some sort of lunatic to even contemplate and then eventually to be participating in this sort of madness. It would have been more intelligent to have brought a bottle of brandy to dispel our misgivings and help propel us into the water or to have just sat on the beach imbibing and enjoying the balmy night air.

The tepid water seemed to calm my nerves as we entered and suddenly we were floating along and the novelty of it all overtook my fears.

The beam, held in one hand by Peter, gave a very good light and the range I would estimate to be in the region of ten paces. Through this shaft of light we could see plenty of marine life as the water was, as usual, very clear. It appeared that the majority of fish were sleeping and only became aroused when we came into close range. The reason that they detected our presence at close proximity seemed to be, not the light, but probably small shock-waves sent through the water by our swimming movement.

Quite a number of fish which do not sleep at night we saw swimming along merrily in the shaft of light. Contrary to our expectations we did not find that the beam mesmerized the fish as a similar beam does to animals in the wilds on land. They either appeared to be oblivious to the light or saw it and kept at a safe distance. The sand sharks certainly saw us from a distance and did their normal camouflage trick of wriggling into the sand for cover.

I had the distinct feeling that behind me where there was no light a predator like a shark or barracuda might make a meal of my flippers or feet or both, and kept glancing behind me. After consultation with Andy, after the event, he said he had experienced the same feeling and had continually glanced behind him as well. The sight of shadowy movements just beyond the range of our light must have prompted these misgivings.

During daylight hours phenomenal colours excite the spear-fisherman on coral reefs, as all gogglers know; but at night all this has gone and the predominant colour is red/brown surrounded by an inky-blackness. Disappointing.

We stayed out for a good two hours or more and basically found after the initial novelty that the lack of colour, the lack of vision and the reaction of the fish was not at all as exciting as daylight goggling. We did, of course, expect to enjoy a bigger bag of fish with greater ease but this was not the case as the light did not mesmerize or attract any numbers of fish. We were surprised and came back with a smaller bag than we would have had during daylight hours.

Flights of fancy

I cannot resist writing about the aircraft and flights during the 1950s. As I said earlier, my job with Gill & Johnson took me to a number of different places in Tanganyika as the quickest method for our Company to move the staff to the clients for audit purposes was to fly. Roads were all very primitive. Distances were great and there seemed to be either landing strips or airfields at almost every corner of the territory.

One of our biggest clients was Balfour Beatty who were building the new harbour at Mtwara and my first flight there was in a De Havilland Dominie biplane which had two engines and carried all of seven of us which made it fully laden. The seats were singly situated , staggered left and right, with a tiny aisle zigzagging up the centre. The passenger on the right in front looked through a doorway with no door, at the pilot who was within touching distance; he was wedged in a tiny compartment on a seat like a sports car with no room to move left or right and therefore remained in his seat throughout the flight. This was very interesting for the front right-hand passenger as he could watch the pilot and see through the windscreen forwards with a vision almost the same as the pilot. Whenever we flew Dominie I muscled my way to this seat.

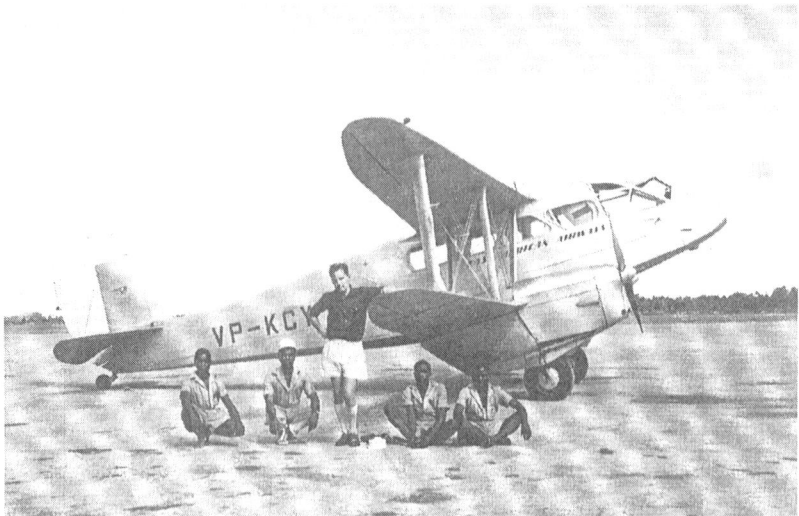

De Havilland Dominie with Tommy Webb and helpers

As this little biplane had a very limited ceiling height it normally used to fly along the coast cruising along at about one or two thousand feet. The view of the beach and coral reefs was absolutely magnificent. The coral islands off the coast between Dar es Salaam and Mtwara are innumerable. At times we could see elephant herds on the left and right of the Lindi/Dar es Salaam road. It was a surprisingly comfortable little plane to fly in as it did not seem to bang, bump and shake as did either the Dakotas or later the Fokker Friendships, which were introduced in the nineteen sixties. I should think it was probably due to the very slow speed at which it cruised along.

On one occasion, coming in to land at Dar on the old landing field at Kurasini, the pilot spotted a young boy in a grassy field who was standing in a position directly underneath our approach flight-path and staring at us intently. Lo and behold the pilot pushed the joystick, (yes a joystick, not a wheel) forward and dipped the nose straight towards the *toto*. I had time to see him duck into a prone position before we swept over him. The pilot looked back at me and grinned. Unfortunately the Dominies were withdrawn to be replaced within a few years of my arrival; their very pleasurable flights ceased in favour of Dakotas and Lockheed Loadstars.

Flying to Mbeya was always a pleasurable trip. We would take off from Dar at the gentlemanly hour of eight or nine a.m. with a first stop at Iringa. About one hour later we took off for Tabora and after another hour, on to Sao Hill where we enjoyed lunch at the Sao Hill Club. At about four p.m. we would touch down at our destination in Mbeya.

Flying in the tropics is normally bad-weather flying as cumulonimbus seem always to build up from nowhere. On our trip with East African Airways on the route I described above the pilot whose aircraft, (Dakotas or Loadstars) would not be able to fly higher than the weather, would duck under the clouds between mountains or high hills. On a few occasions we were so low that I could see the bunches of bananas growing on the trees as we weaved along between high hills or when coming in to land.

There was no flight service in the earlier years of the 1950s but I think the drinking habits of East Africans must have induced East African Airways to introduce coffee, biscuits and latterly sweets for take-off and landing (to clear the ears). One could identify those who were hardly aware that they were in an aircraft, those who were terrified of flying and a large number who appeared to have been pole-axed which of course was the result of a hangover. It was this latter category whom I sometimes joined in sorrow so that EA Airways must have sympathised with us and therefore introduced coffee and biscuits. By the end of some hours of bumping along, landing and taking off and viewing the fascinating countryside, having a delicious lunch at some cool club or hotel, the liver damage seemed to have lessened and one could then look upon life with considerably more enthusiasm.

The entry by air into Mbeya was not easy for the pilot. He had to swoop down through high hills to the airstrip which was near the town in quite a deep hollow. But the Dakotas were up to the task and the excellent pilots were accustomed to twisting and turning into difficult angles on approaches to small landing strips all over East Africa.

The climate of Mbeya is cool and invigorating at an altitude of approximately four to five thousand feet. It was considered to be one of the healthiest climates in Tanganyika and the children who attended the best school in the territory there would return to parents in Dar es Salaam during school holidays with lovely rosy cheeks. Fortunately mosquitoes did not find it healthy at that altitude and therefore Mbeya was free of malaria.

Our transport from the dusty airstrip to the Mbeya Hotel was the normal Land Rover but the journey was short. I would estimate that this hotel was one of the most pleasant in Tanganyika. The rooms, food and service were excellent and the change in climate from the coast was a tonic on its own. The big feature which all remembered afterwards was the fireplace in the lounge. It was a colossal size, lit every evening at all times of the year. Being so big, you could walk under the mantelpiece without bending down and throw a log into the fire. The enormous width had a small seat on each side built into the hearth and one could stand in front, or sit on one of these seats, tankard in hand and enjoy the company of the travellers who were either passing through by air, or travelling south by road to Central Africa or a long way further to South Africa. It was the territory's last outpost on the 'Great North Road' from Cairo to Cape town when travelling south through Tanganyika, close to the Northern Rhodesia border. One can only have an enormous amount of admiration for the pilots of East African Airways at that period of time. The build-up of cumulonimbus over Kenya, Uganda and Tanganyika is very rapid, normally occurring after mid-day. The pilots contended with this ubiquitous hazard with an admirable nonchalance and unassuming attitude, flying Dominees, Dakotas, Loadstars and Friendships and compared to today's modern age and weather technology makes those aircraft seem like dangerous old

Cumulonimbus

flying machines. But the pilot at that time was an expert on geography and had to have a large chunk of intuition – all this over-and-above the normal skills required to fly.

I recall flying from Kisumu to Mwanza, the whole route over Lake Victoria, through a seemingly impenetrable dark black cloud all the way which took about one and a half hours. The plane, a Dakota, was buffeted by high winds and air pockets with rain and hail beating on to it at frequent intervals during the whole flight. I chatted to the pilot after we landed and asked how he had managed to navigate through those conditions. He replied that he flew on beacons but during a few occasions when violent turbulence and lightning upset his instruments he had to rely on intuition until the instruments settled back into operation. He added, "this journey has not been all that bad". I proceeded to the bar in haste and downed a large drink.

In the 1950s the new Dar es Salaam airport was to us a marvellous improvement of modern construction. It had an impressive building with a waving balcony set up on the first floor, (there were only two floors, ground and first), which protruded out and enabled one to greet or wave farewell to passengers arriving or departing. The planes taxied in close to us almost under our noses. We even had a restaurant, bar and lounge behind the waving balcony. There never seemed to be more than one aircraft on the tarmac at any one time and I recall that there was no room for much more.

The main tarmac strip for aircraft to taxi to the airport building was flanked by luscious flat grass fields left and right. Beyond the grass, shrub-like trees.

A crowd of us were seeing off a load of passengers and it was noticed by one spectator that a wild pig was grazing on the grass not far from the taxying strip. The pilot eased the plane forward and the porker stared in indignant defiance at the oncoming intruder. When the plane was fairly close, porky's resolve to stand his ground gave way and he turned and trotted off, and on to the taxying strip in the direction that the plane was travelling. Our hero did not panic and flee at full speed but at a truculent hi-speed trot. The pilot, who had a sense of humour, drove the plane at the pig. It did some wild zigzags as it headed off down the strip with the Dakota following directly behind doing the same zigzags after the pig and gaining ground gradually. After a hundred and fifty yards of this hi-speed pig-trot, porky called it off and veered away towards the shrubbery, turned and looked at the pilot vengefully for a long time and then carried on grazing. All this to the accompanying cheers of the spectators on the waving balcony, half of whom had glasses of ale or stronger stuff in one hand.

The East African wild life bonanza

I had at this early stage in my sojourn in Tanganyika fallen in love with the country. Totally.

It was my intention immediately I knew I was to be living in East Africa, to enjoy the hunting and viewing of all the big game together with the colossal variety of smaller fauna to be found in this unspoilt part of the world.

In the l950s game was so prolific that very large areas were not even protected in Tanganyika. One could hunt in all the areas which were not privately owned or were Royal National Parks. One acquired a rifle for game or a shotgun for birds and ducks. And a licence to hunt. There were limits to the number of each species able to be hunted and certain species which were Royal Game were not allowed to be pursued at all. The latter was usually an endangered species such as chimpanzees, gorillas and a small number of other vertebrates.

There were fees to be paid to the Game Department for each of the bigger game to be bagged. For instance, elephant cost Shs. 200/- each when I first arrived and that was increased to Shs. 400/- in the late l95Os. The annual limit was four. Lions were limited and so were rhino, leopard and a number of other species. Buffalo were not limited and there was no fee to be paid for them.

The situation in Kenya was entirely different as regards hunting areas but the fee for each species was priced and limited to an annual number, as it was in Tanganyika and Uganda. The Kenya Game Department had evolved a marvellous system of block allocation for hunting. The massively vast areas were demarcated into rectangular blocks identified by various boundaries such as "a line drawn between the peak of 'such and such peaks' or 'the road between this village' and that village". It could be a river or a stream. It was however, easy for the hunter to identify comfortably.

Before hunting, the applicant would have to visit the Game Department and book a block which could be identified on a large map in their offices. One did get to know where certain species existed and therefore chose a block in the area in which to hunt. After hunting the hunter would be given a very limited number of days to submit a report (on a form of course), indicating the number and species of game shot. This simple arrangement allowed the Game Department to monitor the number of various species hunted and killed. They also had a staff of experts who counted the game in each block which was done both from the ground as well as from the air. It was efficiently done and enabled a count to be carried out every two or three years. The total number of game species was therefore quite simply calculated in each rectangular block so that if a block became depleted to a lower level than was acceptable for re-stocking, it could then be closed to hunting until the game population bred to a level sufficiently large enough for hunting to re-commence.

In Uganda, the system was totally haywire. One could hunt small game anywhere except in National Parks but to hunt any big game the requirement was that the hunter was obliged to obtain a letter from a Government Minister. To acquire this letter of approval it was necessary to run from one department to another, but unfortunately when the secretary of most Ministers was approached ignorance prevailed and the applicant was told to "come back next week"

I still have a copy of the *Uganda Government Hunting Regulations - Revised Edition of 1964* entitled *'The Game (Preservation and control) Act'* priced Shs. 5/25! The fees for a resident in the regulations of this publication are interesting:

SPECIES	MAXIMUM PER ANNUM	RESIDENT'S FEE
Elephant	2	Shs. 500/-
Lion	1	Shs. 500/-
Leopard	1	Shs. 500/-
Buffalo	6	Shs. 50/-
Crocodile	unlimited	Nil

The above are just a very few of the animals listed. The fees for visitors were double those in the case of elephant and buffalo but for a lion Shs. 500/- and for a leopard Shs. 500/- (the same as residents). At that time the pound was worth Shs 20/- so a resident was not crippled by the fees.

The world of safari - big game hunting

Soon after my arrival in Tanganyika I made enquiries and looked at various weapons from a .22 Savage to double-barrelled .400 side-by-side rifles. In the meantime I purchased an old BSA .22 repeater from an auction. Nice and rusty and only fired when you least expected it! All I could afford!

As time went on I finally decided in 1957 on a medium-sized rifle which was capable of downing the biggest of game but was not too big for using against antelope as well. The .375

48

magnum was and still is, a fine all-rounder but against big game one had to be accurate as the power of impact was minimal when compared to the stopping power of the larger bored rifles upwards of .375. I chose a Fabrique National D'armes De Guerre Herstal Belgique (popularly known as an F.N.) and used it for the next fifteen years. I could rely on it implicitly to fire accurately and not once did it misfire.

My great friend René Vidot bought his rifle a short while after me. It was an old second-hand double-barrel .4OO which had seen many a hunt and we decided to be rather cautious when firing the first few shots. We set up a rough cradle of supports in a low part of a tree with the butt against the trunk. Aimed it as accurately as possible at a sheet of paper with a bulls-eye in the centre and tied a piece of string to the trigger, a long piece of string so that we were about twenty yards away, and pulled. It fired perfectly and we let off five shots without mishap and with very good accuracy.

He used that weapon for elephant hunting for five years before he emigrated to Australia. It never let him down.

Back to my weapon. Well I could not wait to test it as fully as possible on the real thing but I thought it prudent to become accustomed to it on lesser game before being more ambitious. I had met a young Swiss weekend hunter (like myself) and he owned a D.K.W. Jeep four-wheel drive. This was absolutely ideal for hunting and subsequently carried us through terrain in which I never imagined a vehicle would survive. Our first venture was into the bush on the east side of the Dar es Salaam/Morogoro road and about half way to Morogoro. Game was plentiful – zebra, wildebeest, impala, giraffe, hartebeest abounded. Fred had the same calibre rifle as mine and had reconnoitred this area previously. Like me he loved the bush and revelled in this totally uninhabited area where one could enjoy hunting without seeing a single person for hours on end. The type of vegetation was typical of the dry areas away from the coast, medium-height short or low trees with waist-high grass. But very dry and aggressively hot. We hunted during the dry season as these areas were totally impassable during the rainy season. My first shot brought down a handsome-looking wildebeest. This was the beginning of hunting adventures which were to thrill me for the next fifteen years – the solitude, the beauty, the game, the heat, the stalking, the nervous tension before shooting. Yes, I was happy to live in East Africa..

Fred was a big man, well built with rosy cheeks which always gave the impression that he had just come from Europe. He did not ever seem to get sunburnt. We hunted this area four or five times and I enjoyed his companionship and grew to know his habits pretty well, one of which was to bring a brew of black tea laced with sugar and plenty of rum which his wife had prepared together with sandwiches etc for lunch. On our first safari, he tempted me to try this brew after we had munched our sandwiches. He assured me that it was refreshing for hunting bodies in the heat of the day. This, after tramping for miles through the bush! Naively I took a cup of this nectar and fell asleep for a good hour, then awoke with him prodding me with the butt of his rifle.

After these one-day trips to the Morogoro area, we decided to hunt further afield where the bigger game frequented. The Kilombero river is a tributary of the mighty Rufiji and at that time it was able to be approached through Mikumi and then Ifakara. At Ifakara we took to bush tracks and then no tracks and followed the Kilombero up-river for some miles into an area which was wild in the extreme – just nobody; the big river, tall papyrus grass growing on wide flats on either side of the river; a gentle slope rising up from the edges of the papyrus-covered flats to low hills with waist-high grass, shrubs and magnificent thorn trees.

We drove up the gentle slope towards the hills to a viewing position and took in the magnificence of the whole scene. There were elephants, buffalo, wildebeest, zebra, two rhino and a number of small species of game. It was a veritable paradise for animals, what with water, food and no human settlers to poach them or to set up farms and then kill them for stealing their crops. Our mission was not to disturb this splendid sanctuary but to take one or two trophies and then retreat.

We sat and took in this brilliant scene of virgin Africa for some time and peered through our binoculars at the larger tusks and the size of the buffalo horns. There were no tusks of trophy size although we stared for a good hour or two. The buffalo were so numerous that we knew that there must be some elegant bosses amongst the hundreds partly obscured by the tall papyrus grass in which they were moving to and from the water. There was a slight heat-haze from the fierce sun blazing down from a cloudless sky; and because of the big river, considerable humidity. Under the shade of a magnificent spreading thorn tree we viewed this scene with not a little awe.

The trusty DKW took us to higher ground about half way up into the hills where the heat was less intense and the mosquitoes and tsetse-fly not so bothersome. We found a suitable camping position easily and built a fire, put up our little tent, opened the beer and provisionally planned our programme for the following day. To bed early after a meal of bully-beef, thick buttered white bread, tinned peaches and coffee.

The mosquitoes were continually making an entry into our tent although we had a net door near our feet. I could not understand it as I had used this tent before and the mosquito net door had prevented all entry. After about an hour or two, I discovered the reason. Fred was so tall that his feet protruded out of the door and lifted the net giving the mozzies unhindered entry. There were fortunately not a lot of them so I just pulled the blanket over my head and slept soundly. He also pulled the blanket over his head so only had a few bites on his ankles.

The first trophy

We arose early and struck camp, piling all our gear into the DKW. The air was blissfully crisp as we set off but with the anticipation of the day ahead, the thought of the valley heat did not even occur to us. As we descended lower down, that glorious sight of the day before lay in front of us once again and we stopped near the edge of the papyrus. About two hundred yards off hid the jeep and then ourselves and waited. A herd of buffalo was milling around in the papyrus about half way between the water and ourselves but closer to us were approximately eight elephant nosing around and generally creating mayhem amongst themselves.

There were game paths aplenty coming out of the papyrus all along in front of us and to left and right so that we expected perhaps the elephant and more hopefully, the buffalo to come out and provide a clear shot. Fred had decided not to bag anything as big as what we had seen so he left the shooting to me.

The elephant, fortunately, moved closer to the river and the buffalo started to move towards us in order to amble up to the grazing areas in the hills behind us. This was a great moment of tension for me as I studied the horns as they came out of the papyrus. As a complete novice I was tempted to just bag one for experience but Fred gently persuaded me to wait for the latter end of the herd to emerge as he expected the largest horns to be at the rear where the main bull would be keeping an eye on his harem. The wind was only a very gentle breeze and coming from the river. This was ideal as the buffalo has a phenomenal sense of smell. This, combined with telescopic-like eyesight does not give the hunter much of a chance of a close-up shot in open country – and this was very open country between us and the papyrus but we were well camouflaged behind some low bushes with plenty of waist-high grass in front of us, the D.K.W. jeep much further back. The buffalo came closer and closer as we crouched low. I could feel my heart pounding away as I slipped the safety-catch off. Fred was fully loaded and prepared to shoot if we got into trouble. The range decreased as they came towards us and veered slightly to our right. This was even more ideal because, had they headed straight at us, the front end of the herd would have detected us and spoiled any chance of a slow-moving target.

 At this stage I estimated the herd to be well over two hundred and we could smell their distinctive odour as they passed by us towards our right about fifty yards away. Fourth from the end was a rather handsome pair of horns and I steadied my rifle-bead on his shoulder. The kick of a shot from a .375 is quite severe and one must hold the rifle tightly against the shoulder to prevent bruising. I squeezed the trigger. It was not a good shot as I did not allow for the movement forwards of the beast as he walked. The point of entry was just behind the shoulder and he therefore turned and galloped, together with the whole herd back into the papyrus. Although I was fairly sure that the bullet had struck, I did not know where and was mortified to see him not go down. Fred confirmed that he heard the distinctive thud of the bullet impacting. What to do now? Only one thing and that was to go into the papyrus and track him down by following a blood spoor. As the papyrus was approximately ten to twelve feet high and fairly thick, this was not a healthy pastime. We entered slowly, with safety catches off and soon discovered that we could only see about fifteen feet in front of us. My heart was doing all sorts of thumping in my chest again and at least three times just about jumped out of my rib-cage when buffalo, in front of us, heard us coming and charged off, fortunately away from our direction. We had now entered deeper into the thicker papyrus and visibility had reduced in front of us. This was a classic ambush situation. I noticed that Fred had hands that were shaking like a leaf. He seemed to have lead in his boots and continually hung back and sometimes behind me. I urged him to go forward and parallel to me but he soon hung back again and this continued three or four times. His shaking seemed to have increased and it occurred to me that that shaking of hands close to the trigger and behind me was not conducive to a long future for me. In front were the buffalo and behind me, Fred.

However, the dilemma was solved when Fred said he had had enough of this dangerous stuff. The blood trail was not difficult to follow and I was very keen to press on but he advocated we go back and fetch the D.K.W. and drive into the papyrus on the blood spoor. This we did and the marvellous little vehicle pushed straight through the papyrus with ease. It seemed to revel in these conditions although deep elephant-made foot-holes, made during the rains when the ground was muddy, were everywhere. We soon came upon the buffalo lying on its side and stone dead. The shot had entered just behind the shoulder and possibly the heart or some other vital organ. It had run a good hundred and fifty yards into the papyrus before collapsing. I was elated.

 The sheer size of the animal and the good-looking pair of horns were indeed something to behold. The .375 had done its job admirably. The excitement of the preparation, planning, shooting and then the danger of the stalking in the papyrus and finally finding the animal stone dead made up for the lack of a clean shot. I did not begrudge Fred for being so nervous, nor think poorly of him, as I was pretty-well afraid myself but did not show it as he did.

A big task was ahead of us now because, to take the trophy home, the head had to be removed. This proved to be a mammoth operation. The neck of a buffalo is immensely thick and heavy; the skin particularly thick and formidable scalpels like axes and pangas, well-sharpened, are necessary to do the job. It took us at least two hours to complete as our equipment was not as sharp as it should have been. To lift it into the jeep required more effort than one would have thought necessary and the whole operation, in that hot valley, drew perspiration from us so that we were soaked to the skin and sunburnt.

It was a mistake to remove the head at low neck level as it was only the horns and skull that were of value as a trophy when there was no taxidermist within a reasonable distance to stuff head and neck.

As soon as we had emerged from the papyrus, Fred stopped the D.K.W. and we proceeded to remove the head at a level just behind the horns. This took longer than expected and by the time we had finished, dusk was about to descend upon us, so we just set up the tent and built a fire where we were, close to the papyrus.

The day had been a great one for us and for me in particular. We therefore opened the beer and chatted contentedly for a long while in front of the fire before enjoying a bite to eat and then coffee and kip. However, things started to happen around us. The carcass, not more than two hundred yards away had attracted the attentions of the carnivores; and noises from leopard-coughing to lion grunts seemed to get closer and closer. We stoked the fire and put thorn branches over the buffalo head and attempted to retire. The noises became louder and closer and it seemed that an unruly rugger scrum of lions must have been at the carcass. The hyenas were awaiting their chances but also started investigating round our camp. I shone a torch and the inquisitive eyes of hyenas glared back at me.

Fred, who, as I explained before, was of a nervous disposition, stoked the fire into a blaze and it was fortunate that we had gathered a considerable amount of wood before dusk. I crept into the tent, rifle handy and Fred continued frantically to stoke the fire. I was so exhausted that after I had pulled the blanket over my head to keep the mosquitoes at bay, I dropped off to sleep but Fred sat outside and continued to stoke the fire, keeping his rifle next to him. Eventually, quite late and chased by the mosquitoes, he crept into the tent and lay down, blanket over him and feet protruding out of the net door letting a hoard of mosquitoes in. At this level and near the river, the mosquitoes were so thick in the air that at times I thought I was breathing in more mosquitoes than air. I cursed that we had not camped higher up in the hills where the air was fresher with far fewer mosquitoes. As the night wore on, Fred kept going out to make sure that the fire was well ablaze. This let more mosquitoes into the tent and eventually I took my under blanket and the one on top, out to the fire where there were considerably fewer mozzies and slept there the rest of the night, rifle nestling next to me. Fred preferred the tent.

 In retrospect and having had much more experience I know now that the greater danger would have been from the hyenas. The lions were content to enjoy their banquet, with the leopards lurking around the party at a safe distance and hoping for a bite later on, but the irascible hyenas were, as they always are, hungry and dissatisfied with their lot as scavengers. The head of the buffalo must have been an attraction to them; as well as the parts of the neck that were lying around not far from us.

There have been instances, which came to light in later years in the press, of hyenas either biting off the foot or dragging a man and then packing on to him, if he was sleeping next to the fire. Lions have also been known to do the same thing but not, as in our case, if there be food such as a buffalo carcass close by.

The next morning we awoke somewhat the worse for wear - lack of sleep. But Fred, with that fresh pink Swiss complexion, had supplied a succulent meal during the night to hundreds of mosquitoes and his neck had swollen and become very red. Especially at the back and it looked quite alarming. I now quote from the greatest of all European explorers. Henry Morton Stanley wrote in his memoirs *Into the Dark Continent, The travels of Henry Morton Stanley*:

> "where they passed a miserable night for the mosquitoes swarmed and attacked them until morning with all the pertinacity characteristic of these hungry bloodsuckers".

All signs of the carnivores had vanished and fortunately the thorn branches over the trophy had done their work and deterred the hyenas.

We struck camp with a rather depressed looking Fred but he said he had heard of a small mission with a monk, whom he had previously met in Dar es Salaam, who lived close to Ifakara and he wanted to look him up and perhaps he would have something to alleviate the swelling of the neck. We made enquiries at Ifakara and it was easy to find our monk as he was the only missionary in the area and therefore well-known.

The monk lived the life of a hermit in a small dwelling with three Labrador dogs. His residence was jam-packed with books in every nook and cranny. His chapel, or small church was very close by and his mission of converting the heathen must have been a tough assignment but he was, as all Roman Catholic Fathers seem to be, a jolly fellow; overweight and not worried about his situation all alone in the bush – all smiles and full of 'joie de vivre'.

The situation of the cottage in which he lived was at the base of some steep hills and slightly elevated so that he could look out over the plains but the most important asset to his residence was a strong stream which emanated from the hills behind and which flowed right through his back garden. A waterfall poured down into a very deep pool, fast flowing and the water was crystal clear and most pleasant of all, cool, cool, cool in that hot climate. Fred and I at this stage were none too fresh and underarm halitosis must have been creating a strong haze of odious aroma emanating from every pore in our bodies.

Fred complained that my presence was an affront to his smelling buds. I lamented that his perspiration was far worse than the smell of a polecat. We took our soap and towels and then plunged into that blissfully cool water, wallowing like hippos for a long time before and after soaping ourselves.

3

Zanzibar

During my first year I played tennis mainly, golf once and joined the Dar rugger team which held practices and matches at the Gymkhana Club. It was a scrappy team of rugby enthusiasts and a lot of fun was had playing on Saturday afternoons. Normally the teams A and B or just mixed, with at least half of the players suffering hangovers from Friday night before, would play in the cool season but even then it was a pretty warm climate in which to play rugger. It also enabled one to work up an extra thirst for a night at the Ocean Breeze nightclub.

I was injured during a match and went into the European Hospital where it was decided that the cartilage of my left knee should be removed. In those days there was no rising out of bed allowed for ten days after the operation and one could just lie back and enjoy the attentions of the nursing sisters. I just relaxed, read books and flirted with as many of the nurses as possible. It was with reluctance that I was finally discharged but I had no option as the operating surgeon, a Mr Howett, declared that I was fit enough to go home. Bad sport. But a fine surgeon.

My employers Gill and Johnson and with Jim Storey as Manager, allowed me to take ten days sick leave after leaving hospital. I decided to go to Zanzibar, where I had not been before and took the first flight to this island which was ruled by the Sultan of Zanzibar. The Dakota descended towards the coconut-palmed coral-based green oasis in the Indian Ocean and I could see how clever the Arabs had been in settling centuries before, into this jewel of the coastal islands of East Africa.

I booked into the Zanzibar Hotel and soon could not help nosing around the precincts admiring something which was completely new to me, Arab architecture and culture. I was fascinated by the Arabs themselves as I had never seen or been in contact with many before this. At that time, Zanzibar was a duty-free port and items such as cameras, binoculars, watches etc were considerably cheaper than on the mainland. I bought a Voigtlander for Shillings two hundred and fifty. It was a marvellous buy and it is now an antique which I still have and which continues to take excellent pictures.

All the men wore long white Arab-type robes with colourful turbans and many had belts with daggers or large keys hanging from their belts. Most sported long beards and all wore sandals; they had furtive and sometimes arrogant looks on their faces. A number of them were camera-shy and would walk away. The only visible parts of the women were of course eyes through a slit in the head-dress, and sandalled feet. They also smelt of perfume. The presence of Allah seemed to lurk everywhere. But his nose was somewhat put out of joint by the overwhelming presence of the perfume of the cloves. I had never experienced the aroma before and I think Zanzibar is one of the few places in the world where the clove thrives and where the air is filled with this delicious scent.

It was an easy walk, or hobble for me with one knee still only half operative, to all the parts of the town centre, the Sultan's Palace and the beach. I therefore wandered through the narrow streets which were so narrow that no motorcar could travel. Only pedestrians, except for one short one-way street for cars. As Zanzibar was a stop for passenger-ships all the little Arab *dukas* catered for the tourist trade. Brass coffee jugs, cups, jewellery, ivory carvings and trinkets; clothes, watches, cameras, copper trays and of especial interest were the highly decorative Arab chests. Before leaving Dar es Salaam I was advised to have a suit made in Zanzibar as these were made by tailors who abounded everywhere and the suits were very well tailored and very cheap. As the ships normally stopped for only a day the tailors had geared themselves up for measurements in the morning, fitting at lunch-time and collection of completed garment mid-afternoon. All ready in less than one day!

I wandered into one of Zanzibar's Saville Row tailoring houses, selected material which was a very pale tropical-type light-weight, went through the antics of measurement-taking, later fitting and finally took delivery – all in the same day. The bubbly Arab tailor seemed over-the-moon with admiration when he looked at it on me but when I looked in the mirror I had grave doubts about his credentials. It seemed to bulge in the wrong places and too tight where it should be loose but he assured me that this was the latest fashion! None of the tailors would start the job unless fully paid in advance so I took it and walked out with some misgivings about Allah's devotees. A week later when I had arrived back in Dar I wore it, and became drenched in a shower of rain which was not a heavy one, but the effect on the suit was startling. I have never seen material shrink like that. The trouser-legs rose to ankle height and the sleeves shrunk to way above my watch strap so that if I stretched my arms one could almost see elbows. The jacket would not button up, the fly – only just. Ah well, it lasted a week!

It was a stop-start progress when walking along these narrow streets with little *dukas* on either side. To the newcomer all was interesting and as one stopped or slowed down to see some article, the shop-owner would tug at one's sleeve in an attempt to steer the onlooker inside the shop and make a sale. Coffee vendors were plentiful and I partook of a cup on a few occasions but it was thick black stuff with no milk and plenty of sugar, or no sugar. Only Allah knew where the coffee grains came from.

The Sultan of Zanzibar had decreed many generations before that water was God's (or probably Allah's) gift from heaven and should not therefore be sold but given away free. Water was plentiful on the island and therefore not only did the people on the island not pay for water, nor did the ships. Consequently all the shipping passing close to Zanzibar stopped to fill water tanks and it was the passengers from the liners that enabled the profitable tourist-trade to be built up and to flourish to a degree that tourism became one of the mainstays of the island's booming economy.

Zanzibar was prosperous. Sultans had ruled for centuries and prided themselves on the wellbeing of the inhabitants. The ruling class Arabs were in the minority and the Africans were, even after slavery was abolished, basically 'hewers of wood and fetchers of water'. Very well treated but not as equals. Arabic and Swahili were the respective languages and the Africans prided themselves on speaking the most pure Swahili in East Africa. A boast which was disputed by the mainland coast Swahilis. The Sultan's Palace was an impressive example of ancient Arab architecture and I

The Sultan's palace

photographed it from a number of angles. The second day after I arrived I was holed up in the bar of the hotel and I met an expatriate inhabitant who immediately befriended me. He seemed a trifle lonely, waiting for his wife to arrive from the UK and occupied a spacious apartment on the first floor of one of the buildings in the town centre. He very kindly invited me to share his accommodation for the rest of my stay. Although the Zanzibar Hotel was fascinating as an Arabic relic, I was fortunate to now be able to live in an Arab dwelling, even though the interior furnishings were western style.

The front door was one of those ornately carved doors with the extraordinarily simple lock mechanism found on all the traditional dwellings. A heavy wooden sliding plank was mounted on the inside of the door and slid left to right or vice-versa through old iron-fashioned decorative hoops when the oversized key was inserted and turned from the outside. The key was massive, often nine inches to one foot in length and shaped to fit only that steel tumbler bolted to the plank inside that particular door. The walls on old town Zanzibar buildings were the thickest I have ever seen. No windows, just wooden shutters. The street was so narrow that one could almost shake hands with the inhabitants on the opposite side. On the first floor the windows were so positioned that all was private and one could not peer into the dwelling on the other side of the street or alley.

Carved Zanzibar door

My host and friend David, (cannot remember his surname), invited me to the Club for a look at his second waterhole, the first being the Zanzibar Hotel. It was a fine old colonial club with an active bar. During the evening he introduced me to a lovely young lady whose name I also cannot remember but she was the wife of the number two at the British Embassy. I was not aware of this. Hubby must have been at the bar as we were sitting at a table out in the cooler air on the verandah.

Meeting the same old people, night after night at the Club or Hotel made the small European community on the island eager to meet and converse with visitors and I found that she was keen to show me around the Zanzibar places of interest. She went everywhere by bicycle and somehow located one for me the following day.

I could not keep my fingers off my new camera and she took me to all the beauty spots and places of interest. There was no harbour for ships in Zanzibar and they would therefore anchor in deep water near the beach but there was a dhow jetty and quite a large dhow harbour. This attractive young lady took me and my camera to the dhow harbour and I could see that she was a frequent visitor as the locals greeted her heartily as she rode along the little wharf near the rows of anchored dhows. She always bought her fish there she said. I took shots. Then on to the market with her telling me all about the interesting parts as we rode along. During my stay she took me to the coconut groves, the outstandingly white sandy beaches where we swam and she collected shells which were able to be seen quite easily in the waist-deep, gin-clear water.

The centuries-old graves were an island attraction and I photographed these most ornate and colourful tombs. The old slave market was visited so were the clove plantations. She took me everywhere. Some years later I was to meet an old East African hand who had been present at the Zanzibar Slave Market during its last few years of operation.

Old Arab tomb

Zanzibar slave market

My stay in Zanzibar was somewhat of a drinking spree staying with David and him being an enforced bachelor and me with no ties. But during sober hours I was captivated by Zanzibar island and this young lady, who was, by the way a few years older than I and a most pleasant guide. I never met hubby, praise Allah.

Having bought a camera, suit and suitably rewarding David with a few bottles of sustenance my funds had dwindled and I found I did not have sufficient *shillingi* for my air-fare back to Dar es Salaam. What now? No passenger ships to Dar nor any regular passenger sea service and me due to start work in two days' time on Monday. David said he thought that the dhows took passengers but knew of no one who had done the voyage.

During the monsoon winds the dhows would arrive from two sources – India and Arabia, or the Gulf States as it is known today. Those from India would have a ballast of Mangalore tiles which would be in great demand for the roofs of the houses in East Africa. They would also carry all sorts of cheap bric-a-brac, beaten brassware, silverware, metal ware, beads etc. Furthermore the dhow provided an almost risk-free entry for the illegal immigrants from India and the Middle East. Ordinary smuggling was commonplace.

The dhows from Arabia carried Persian carpets, leather ware etc and of course illegal immigrants but not as many illegal immigrants as from India as the Arab was generally satisfied to be living with his folk in Arabia and regarded East Africa as a remote outstation where Allah was not held in such high esteem as he should be. However, I must say that the Arabs had a great following amongst the coastal African tribes and Allah (or Mohamed if he was greater, who knows?) was revered. This was all as a result of centuries of Arab presence in East Africa and particularly so on the coast where the slave trade flourished until the early part of this century. Swahili is full of Arabic.

When returning from East Africa the dhows would carry mangrove poles, ivory and in the old days - slaves.

Upon enquiry at the dhow harbour I found that I could travel to Dar es Salaam for the princely sum of *shillingi kumi* (ten bob) and that a vessel was leaving that Saturday afternoon. Time? Well as soon as Allah willed? I semi-hobbled (getting better now after all the bicycle riding) back to the apartment, packed my single suitcase and proceeded to the harbour and found my transport. It was quite a handsome-looking craft and as I boarded I found that I was actually looking forward to the trip.

Within an hour we had left the harbour and started to chug along on the power of a small motor. The fascinating island of Zanzibar started to fade away and I had time to look around. Our cargo was mainly men, women, children, goats, sheep and a couple of calves and yes, some chickens – always present in East Africa, even on the sea. I was told that the hold held coconut fibre from Zanzibar and some Persian carpets but these were covered and I could not see them. The length from stem to stern I would estimate to have been about forty to forty-five feet. Most of the passengers of maybe thirty in total preferred to stay with the goats and sleep on the lower deck. When I went down to have a look I found the aroma to be almost lethal and therefore hastily retreated back to the open deck above. There was a small wheelhouse amidships just to the rear of the mast. The *nahoda* (skipper) had a bunk to sit on just behind the wheel.

The weather was balmy and it was a lovely evening as we chugged westwards towards the mainland.

Just before dusk a gentle breeze came up and the skipper switched off the motor and raised the lateen-rigged sail. The crew was two plus **skipper** and so being gaff-rigged just two men raised the whole sail on a pulley-block mounted at the top of the mast whilst the skipper held the sheet at the lower front end until the crew, after securing their halyard came and secured what the skipper was holding. I have always looked at a lateen-rigged set-up and thought "how simple" and now this large sail had been set up by just three men.

Lateen rig (sail)

We sailed along serenely at a slow pace and all was peaceful except that half of the passengers had at this stage seemed intent on turning themselves inside out. I noticed that it was mainly the women who were prone to sea-sickness. Only a few men and almost none of the children. The animal life seemed unperturbed and appeared to be seasoned sailors.

Ten shillings for upper deck, I don't know what they paid below, from Zanzibar to Dar es Salaam. I thought upon leaving that the menu might not be substantial so I had armed myself with a beer, a soft drink and half a loaf of bread. My prudence was rewarded as there was nothing except suspect-looking water from a grotty-looking wooden barrel if one tipped it over. Others lit primus stoves and cooked things which looked good but smelled revolting. Have you ever smelt a sheet of dried fish being heated with some rice and lentils over a primus stove? A blob of ghee thrown in to lubricate the brew!

I was thankful for the *nasseem* (gentle breeze) and remained upwind of the cooking and watched the skipper navigating his way. Navigate? All he had was the wheel. I never saw a compass and he told me that he kept one to comply with the law. It was stowed away below decks.

He was an elderly gentleman with a beard, *kanzu*, wide belt, sandals and turban. All workmanlike-looking and nothing flashy about him. The passengers soon started to lay their blankets out on the deck as darkness overtook but it was a long time before I was able to go to sleep. It crossed my mind that if, after the sun had gone down, the skipper had reversed direction, none of us would be any the wiser until morning when the sun rose again and we might be half way to mother India or Arabia. However, he looked to me like a reasonable rogue so I went to sleep with some clothes from my suitcase for a pillow.

As the sun started rising on a beautiful day so the cacophony started. Prayer mats were dug out of rolls or bags, laid out facing eastwards and Allah was supplicated, revered, placated, esteemed, etc. etc. Well Allah must have been pretty chuffed at that lot as they carried on for an awful long time. The women took no part in this. Eventually, and I mean eventually, because even the skipper and crew had a go, the wailing piped down.

Next on the agenda was breakfast and something else I had not bargained for. Let's start with the breakfast, the same old thing again as last night but re-heated and at that time of the morning, smelled as though the period of night-time had had its effect in that balmy air and now a fermented brew of fish, rice, lentils, ghee and a spot of curry powder added, was pervading the air. I became alarmed when the skipper accepted some of this gunge as land was not in sight and I thought if I or anybody else had to steer to Dar es Salaam it would be most difficult without the compass. Ah but it was not to be as the constitution of the skipper must have been iron-clad. All he did after eating was to belch loudly a number of times with a look of relish on his face and sail on serenely.

What I had not bargained for or even thought about was the natural functions of the body. I was soon to discover the niceties of this operation, aboard this liner. There was a box of wooden planks with three sides, no top, but a floor of sturdy wooden planks and in this floor a round hole approximately twelve inches in diameter. This box was secured at deck-level on the top deck to the side of the *dhow* and jutting outwards over the edge above the water. The side planks reached up to about a point between thighs and waist and so one walked on to this long drop in full sight of all those on deck, dropped garments which come down or hitched up garments to waist level if they were donned from the top. There was no door leading into it, so all and sundry viewed the proceedings.

I took my turn and growled at the kids who were awaiting theirs in the queue. They grinned at me. Thank goodness it was not some fat female devotee of Allah who was next in the queue after the kids. If that had been the case it would have been less embarrassing to dive over the edge and swim for Dar, regardless of sharks. During mid-afternoon we entered Dar es Salaam Harbour with sail down and motor running. With the exception of the box-reclining, squatting long-dropping, whatever one wants to call it; it was an unforgettable experience which was most enjoyable. The palms around the harbour entrance and the aroma of the spices as we entered made me feel at home again. How gorgeous!

Arab dhow

4

New Horizons

As I mentioned earlier, Gill & Johnson imported me from South Africa to Dar es Salaam in April l95l. I worked for them for two years with some sort of notion of returning to Cape Town to qualify, when Singer Sewing Machine Company offered me a job with a much more lucrative position and with every two to three years UK leave. This was comparable to the level of all the other expatriates. My previous employers only offered me 'long leave' to South Africa and as I had never been to Europe before, I was keen to see the UK and the northern hemisphere. It was natural, therefore, that I jumped at this opportunity. I enjoyed the next fifteen years working for Singers. Dar es Salaam for five years, Nairobi for four years, Kisumu for twenty-two months, back to Nairobi for two years and finally Kampala for two years.

Singers were a great company (at that time the thirteenth biggest company in the world) and our business over the whole of East Africa was enormous with ninety-five per cent of our trade supplying the village tailors who, with a treadle sewing machine, made all the clothes for the local population. These customers were sold machines from one hundred and twenty-eight Singer shops scattered throughout Kenya, Tanganyika, Uganda and Zanzibar. Each shop had a staff of: a Manager, Assistant Manager, two Clerks and a Saleslady, together with a group of Field Salesmen. The Manager was supplied with a vehicle (Singer Van or in deep bush areas, a Land Rover).

I started off as the accountant in our Dar es Salaam office which was the Head Office for Tanganyika and answerable to Singers in Paris, France.

At the end of l952 an event occurred that was to change the rest of my life. Dar es Salaam had a large number of colonial servants, commercial employees and a few local entrepreneurs. All were career orientated and men who had been in East Africa for a number of years, married with families, returning to England every two to three years on 'long-leave' but also entitled to two weeks 'local leave' annually. As a result of these ex-patriot employees there were a number of children being educated in the very good schools existing in various parts of East Africa, but particularly in Nairobi where the High Schools were situated. There was also a large proportion of young people recently having just finished school and working in local positions such as secretaries or receptionists. The Gymkana Club was well-frequented by all these young people whereas the parents were more inclined to join the Dar es Salaam Club which was much more expensive. The Dar es Salaam Yacht Club consisted of both categories – old and young. I was a member of both the Gymkhana Club and the Yacht Club, as I enjoyed both tennis and 'messing around in boats'.

During this time I caught sight of a most lovely creature – her name, I took pains to find out, was Cynthia Shead. My great friend René Vidot had recently married Helen who worked, by a marvellous coincidence, in the same office of Income Tax as Cynthia. At my instigation, René and Helen arranged a meeting and I was immediately captivated. She was not only

Our marriage at St Alban's Church, Dar es Salaam with Cynthia signing the register aided by Archdeacon Capper

glamorous but spoke English perfectly as did most of the young girls from UK, and also had impeccable manners. I pursued her relentlessly. Yes, I hoped she would accept my proposal of marriage. She did. After an engagement of eight months we were married in St. Alban's Church in Dar es Salaam by Archdeacon Capper. She was, and still is, after fifty years of marriage, bubbly and glamorous. Cynthia's parents, Ernest and Ivy, were long standing expatriates and she had a younger brother Anthony still at school in Kongwa. Ernest, known as Ernie, was due to retire and immediately after our marriage at the end of l954, the family returned to England to settle in Teignmouth, South Devon, taking Anthony with them to finish his schooling.

Our first-born appeared a year later named Graham Barry and three years after that, John Hilton was born. The babies were both born in the European Hospital in Dar es Salaam. My parents came from South Africa for a holiday with us and to look after Graham and myself whilst Cynthia was hospitalised for the birth of John. I was transferred to Nairobi in l958 and this was the beginning of a long period of time when we breathed, savoured, enjoyed and revelled in the absolutely sublime climate of Nairobi and its surrounds. After Dar es Salaam the air was like champagne. However, we were not unhappy with the heat of Dar where the babies were brought up with barely nothing more than a vest and pants, as it was so hot day and night. Houses had no air-conditioning in those days.

Haven of Peace was absolutely idyllic for a young family. We bought a house in Kurasini and moved into it straight after our honeymoon. It had a *makuti* roof but a standard type structure of bricks and mortar and a comfortable-sized garden which was totally neglected. Three lovely palm trees were the only plants. The building society would not finance the house unless I roofed it with tiles so I arranged to have the replacement done immediately upon our return from honeymoon.

My company – Singers per kind manipulating of my boss, Karl Heine - loaned me a brand-new long wheelbase Land Rover for our honeymoon to Magamba and Lushoto. A most generous gesture seeing that I had been employed by them for only two years. Our first night was spent in the Morogoro Hotel after setting out from Dar es Salaam at about four pm and stopping and drinking a bottle of champagne (given to us by my boss) whilst looking down at Dar es Salaam and the sea from the hills which surround the town. Then fifty-two miles on – the Morogoro Hotel for the night. What a dump!

En route to honeymoon

After a long, hot, dusty trip of one hundred and fifty miles from Morogoro towards Lushoto the road starts to climb steeply into the Usambara mountains and takes one to the *Magamba Country Club*, or rather, it used to be, as the Club was turned into a Mission Station a few years after our stay there. Crisp, cool air in mountainous surroundings with log fires every night, marvellous food and the Manager having given us the best suite (*rondavel* en-suite with blazing fire). A lively and attractive cosy bar served the twenty-or-so residents.

We spent a week of sheer bliss there and then proceeded to Lushoto to a fascinating guest-house called Heidi's (I think), on a coffee *shamba* owned by a German farmer and his wife. This enabled me to look at the workings of a coffee farm which I had not seen before. There were a number of Germans in Tanganyika as they had also discovered the magic of East Africa during the first World War (Tanganyika was a German colony before World War One) and continued to stay although Britain had now ruled for many years up to l954.

Our hosts were still totally German and lovely people. Their house and the *rondavels* were furnished as though they still lived in Germany and we were introduced, in their dining-room, to a dumb waiter, the largest we have ever seen, with two layers, and this convinced us to acquire one, one day. The food was as solid and tasty and good as all Germans normally provide. We put on weight needless to say and twenty-five years later we eventually acquired a dumb waiter ourselves, which we still have to this day.

After using my two weeks' annual (local) leave on our honeymoon we returned to Dar. The roof contractors started

Our house in Dar es Salaam

to convert the *makuti* to mangalore tiles within a month of our return. What a mess! The rain had held off for about a week and a half whilst the tiles were being put in place over the front rooms of the house. Our bedroom was towards the back and it was rather pleasant to look up at the stars where the tiles were yet to be placed, whilst going to sleep. You guessed it, a big big storm blew up and it rapidly started to bucket down on us during the dead of night. We had moved most of the furniture to the covered rooms but there was no room for our bed there. I grabbed raincoats and threw them over our three-quarter-size bed and we huddled under the covers with drips of rain seeping into every nook and cranny of the insufficiently covered bed. Who remembers those heavy tropical downpours and thunderstorms that periodically hit the East African coast? Most of you who lived in that area of the tropics for any length of time will know exactly what I mean. In no time the floor of cement had become three inches deep in water and I peeped over the side to see our slippers floating away merrily on a rapidly-moving stream. What a lovely way to start a marriage! I don't know why Cynthia did not leave me *mara moja*. (immediately). We lived in that house for a further four years before moving to Nairobi. We improved it by building an extra bedroom and a patio with pergola, extending out from the French doors of the lounge. The Varcoes, our neighbours, became great friends; he was an architect and partner in the firm of Cobb, Archer, Scamell and Lambert.

Week-ends, Alex (Varco) who was about ten years older, would come spear-fishing with us to the islands and although I considered him 'old', he would keep up with us admirably.

We soon held some pretty hectic parties as only East Africans can and I rapidly found out that my rather serious neighbour would become the life and soul of the party after a few drinks. I mean, to see him dancing with my wife, or his, with a pair of rubber flippers for goggling on his feet and a Red-Indian feather head-dress, with him continually pushing his spectacles from half-way down his nose back to his eyes, was a sight worth seeing. Where he kept the headdress between parties and where he acquired it was a mystery to me and it seemed to be quite genuine. He had previously been employed by Dunlop in Brazil and perhaps acquired his feathers there but he would never say. What a character; we missed them when we moved to Kenya.

To bring up a family in Dar es Salaam had a few drawbacks but on the whole it was an ideal place for the children to enjoy. We were very lucky that in the early formative years the first two, Graham and John, were able to enjoy the proximity of the sea and as they grew older we were able to send them to good East African schools in Nairobi.

The East African beaches are by far the best in the world. When one considers hundreds of miles of broad clean white sandy beaches, totally unpolluted with anything as obnoxious as oil, humans or litter; the tepid water, as clear as a bell with palm trees ever present near the high-tide mark, the coral reefs, marvellous shells, then it all adds up to what we became quite accustomed to – total bliss for swimming and picnicking, and sunbathing.

The history of the East African coast line is as ancient as most of the historical sites of the world, with ruins of ancient cultures dotted at intervals from Lindi in the south-east of Tanganyika to Lamu in the north-east of Kenya. Gedi in Kenya, between Kilifi and Malindi, only a few yards from the sea shore is possibly the best-known and one of the best preserved. During the early 1960s when we visited this ruin and there was no guard, no fence, no fee to pay and it was completely deserted – not a soul except Cynthia, myself and the two boys – very quiet except for the odd buzzing insect and the rustle of leaves high up in the trees. It was quite extensive and well-preserved, very eerie due to the lack of humans and totally silent, covered by lovely big trees to shade everything. A gentle breeze would come from the sea which cooled us down from the mid-day heat. Rumour had it as the one-time seat of the Queen of Sheba. Archaeological scholars, since that time, will have probably found more likely solutions as to the founders of this fascinating spread of ruins. We had to hold on tightly to the boys as a large deep well came to light, totally unfenced, and could have presented a huge disaster.

Near Bagamoyo, north of Dar es Salaam were some old ruins, which we visited. They consisted mostly of old Arab tombstones and graves. Some of the graves were covered with low concrete crumbling walls and roofs; when one entered in a crouching position or on all fours, bats by the dozen would fly out in all directions but some would remain hanging on the ceilings, fast asleep. Not a place for the women, who imagine that a bat has one great ambition and that is to nest in their hair.

Now let us look a little further at the beaches. One could take a picnic and select a place quite easily and not far from Dar es Salaam, which would be absolutely deserted, beautiful and safe to swim in. The sand was all of a fine texture and pure and clean, almost white. Normally we would go with another family and the children would all have the time of their lives digging in the sand, walking on the coral reef at low tide or swimming in the tepid water at high tide. The men, and some of the more adventurous ladies would go out at high-tide spear-fishing with snorkels, spear-fishing gun, flippers and goggles. This was a more leisurely type of fishing for the men but we always returned with crayfish although not always with fish. On many occasions we went out without spear-guns and just enjoyed gazing at the truly wonderful underwater world of sea-life, coral, colours, gently waving seaweed, multi-coloured small fishes of which there were thousands, not forgetting the larger species, also those of strange colours and shapes. Of course there were many many shells on the sea-bed and in the clear East African Indian Ocean waters one could collect the beautiful larger cowrie shells and clam (I think you call them that) shells with fingers poking out from the edges.

Naturally our picnic pack contained cold drinks and beer for the men and towards evening one could relax and enjoy the most beautiful sunsets in the world. All predominately red with large columns of lighter and darker shades of red blending with a silver-edged lining and perhaps some dramatic cumulo nimbus rising from low down ready to travel to us overnight to give us a good downpour and cool down the air.

Both of our boys, Graham and John, learnt to swim in the sea. Swimming pools were almost non-existent in Dar es Salaam but what did we need them for? With waters and beaches like we had, a swimming pool was superfluous.

At times there would be *madafu* sellers and it was always a pleasure to buy a coconut, ready holed for drinking, from the smiling seller for a few cents. It had its own *madafu* flavour and the coconut kept it cool. To watch a *toto* or 'boy' scaling a tree to pick the unripe coconut was always intriguing. No rope or safety harness and with a dexterity that was truly breathtaking, he would scale the palm tree, clinging on with hands and feet climbing to the upper foliage, unhinge the coconut and drop it and then return down with a big smile. I never heard of any accidents to these climbers. Usually an old man would be the vendor and slice the top off the unripe green coconut – with a very sharp *panga* with accurate skill so that a round clear drinking hole would enable the purchaser to have easy access to a lovely drink. Some of our forward thinking pals would remember to bring a bottle of gin along and pour a tot into the coconut to make a 'coconut-gin' cocktail.

The Africans believed that a coconut would not drop on one's head because it looked down at you through its eyes. On a coconut, opposite the position where it is attached to the tree by a stem, are three dark round inset patches about half an inch in diameter and placed fairly close together in a triangle. As these are its 'eyes' the Africans believe that one can walk or sleep under coconut palms without fear of the nut falling on to one's head and injuring or maiming or killing anybody!

Before I joined Singers and when I worked for Gill and Johnson, I was sent to Tanganyika Packers to take part in an audit. Whilst discussing the tins of meat with the Sales Manager, the subject of labelling on tins came up. He told us that some years previously, the label on the tin was an *ngombe* (cow or ox). Sales had been steady but not exciting and therefore during a meeting of all those involved in selling, a suggestion was put forward that the label be changed. It was decided that a new more self-revealing label be printed and affixed to the tins. But what? After a prolonged sales meeting it was decided that the Africans would be impressed if they knew that the meat in the tins was so good and tasty that all the whites ate it and thrived on it.

In their wisdom the 'powers that be' in Tanganyika Packers had a label printed which illustrated a distinguished looking *bwana* with topee, red cheeks and rather elderly-looking. Distinctive grey moustache. In other words – a wise elder of robust appearance, full of health. Within a month sales plummeted. Naturally pandemonium broke out in the office of Packers. What to do? Spies were bundled out in haste and came running back, all with the same story. The customers would not eat the meat inside 'those' tins as they assumed that they contained the meat of the *bwana* on the label! *Ngombe* (cattle) labels were re-instituted. Sales and life reverted to normal. Tranquillity once more.

In East Africa there was a large number of folk who were not just numbers but tremendous 'characters'. To explain briefly - there were those who were in East Africa who just loved the country, others who had decided to definitely remain for the rest of their lives in their chosen careers. A few who came to make a quick buck and return to the UK and buy a house and remain there. Some who loved African and Arab cultures. There were those young rakes who lived for the attentions of the lovely young ladies. The hunters of the bush who loved the sheer beauty or miles and miles of untamed country and the abundance of wild life. Plenty who loved the taste of alcohol which was very cheap, whisky at threepence a tot. Great characters in Government who were dedicated and formidable country-lovers and country builders – keen to further the education and advancement of the local Africans. What about those who had gone bush, one of whom I described earlier by the name of 'Rufiji'. And then we had a few who were escaping the law (from misdeeds in other countries) but who soon reverted to their old tricks and were caught up by our own *serikali* (police). Sometimes. The Greek community was large and almost entirely consisted of settlers, some over several generations – sisal plantation owners, hoteliers, all wheelers and dealers with a great penchant for spotting good business opportunities. A large number of them were extremely wealthy and worked hard.

My own father-in-law, Ernie Shead, was employed by East African Railways and Harbours earlier as an accountant and then switched over to catering as he had had prior experience in hotel management in Uganda. He originally went out to East Africa in 1927, without a job, found one and lived the rest of his life there retiring in 1954, to Teignmouth, Devon. Unfortunately a retiring and sedentary style of living in his retirement could not have suited his health very well as he died at the age of fifty-nine in 1964. A truly fine gentleman of a gentle nature and distinguished looks who loved East Africa and in particular, the fishing for Nile Perch on the river Nile at Namasagale when he was stationed at Kampala.

It was at this time in my life in 1958 that I decided to settle in East Africa permanently. I could not think of any other place in the world that would suit me after having spent seven years in Tanganyika and seen a good deal of Kenya.

Not only was I happy to change my allegiance to this country and live permanently here but my company Singers was urging me to adopt a British passport.

My ancestors were based in Kelso, Scotland for centuries and I therefore considered a British passport to be the most natural allegiance to which I could adapt. I might add that my grandfather contracted tuberculosis and was advised by doctors in Kelso to take a voyage around the world to possibly shake off the TB. He had just completed his articles and qualified as a chartered accountant. He undertook the voyage in a sailing ship in 1880. The ship docked at Cape

Town on its first leg. During the stopover there, he heard of a dry, dry situation where sufferers of TB could spend time and recover from the disease. He therefore left the ship and travelled to and settled in Cradock in the middle of the Karoo in the Cape. He must have recovered as he lived to the ripe old age of 81!

The change to British nationality was only natural and I was proud to become a British citizen in the late 1950s.

The author 1951

5

Characters and incidents

Well let me start off with **Jack Smith**. I was on safari after buffalo and not far from Kibereri. We had seen no sizeable herds and although I had picked up a tracker (so-called; one took a chance when engaging one of these boys as they all claimed to be trackers just to get a ride and some meat), had not enjoyed any success but was told of a resident crocodile hunter, a *bwana* who lived on the Ruaha River. After some enquiries, I found a disused bush track for vehicles which eventually led to his residence. He was completely bush, (shunned civilization). Had been for more than ten years and loved it. His residence, two papaya-grass rondavels only yards from the river which was actually a small tributary of the Ruaha. There were a number of immature crocodile skins in various positions close by to the rondavels. Immensely large shade-trees towered over the rondavels and smaller 'drying' trees which kept everything cool. I discovered from him that it was imperative to keep the skins in the shade whilst curing. He explained that his situation was never flooded by the river as it was only a small tributary of the Ruaha. It gave him access to the big river as the confluence was only half a mile away and he could travel there by canoe and do his hunting, always at night.

 The clothes that adorned him were just a *kikoi* and a pair of sandals. A *kikoi* is a brightly coloured wrap-around covering the torso from chest to thighs. He spoke well with a strong mid-English accent and was pleased to tell me all about the life he was leading. He had not seen civilization for probably a 'couple' of years or more, could not remember exactly how many and was not interested in returning. No radio, and just basic African-type food – posho, tea, mboga, rice and venison. He had his own home-brewed pombe and never moved from this area. All skins were bought by an Indian trader once every few months and this trader would bring him supplies of the above-mentioned groceries and bags of rock salt and saltpeter for skin treatment and ammunition for his .375 Magnum rifle (the same size as mine).

I asked about malaria as he seemed to be rather thin and a little sallow. His answer was that he had had it frequently but managed to subdue it with regular small doses of quinine. He enjoyed having three wives and claimed that that was what kept him trim. Whew, strong man!

As I earlier mentioned, most of his skins were of immature crocodiles. He explained that the young smaller skins were of a softer and better quality than the fully-grown models, consequently fetching a much higher price.

Well, so much for Jack Smith, a totally relaxed and contented human being with not a care in the world.

During my early years in Dar es Salaam as a bachelor I met a young bank clerk **Norman Salvage** originally from South Africa. Norman was an unassuming hard-working clerk in the Standard Bank. At parties it was a different matter. He would, after a few drinks, wake up and take charge so that the party was never in danger of being dull. Naturally very popular but I was inclined to be wary of him. He had a habit of leading one astray with admirable ease. I knew that if I joined him at a bar one thing would lead to another. The result – a hangover.

What comes to my mind about Norman was, as a conscientious bank clerk one would hardly expect an heroic deed from him. I was wrong.

A newspaper article appeared in the *Standard* of a leopard being stabbed to death by the friend of a hunter when the hunter was being mauled. The newspaper article was glowing with accolades of bravery by Norman Salvage.

Kay Knott, a lifelong friend of our family and a nursing sister who assisted in the birth of our first-born, Graham, was a very close witness of the whole episode. I inveigled her into telling me all about it. This was in 2002 when I started to write these recollections.

It is best that I now give her written account of this heroic and fearful event.

She writes – "my first visit to a game reserve was a very dramatic affair and almost ended in tragedy. Andy and myself went with another couple to a game reserve some two hundred miles inland near the small town of Morogoro. We stayed with a friend overnight and retired early in order to be up and on our way before dawn.

A game hunter called for us very early next morning and drove us to the reserve, in his land rover. We reached there just as dawn was breaking. It was all very exciting especially for me as I had only seen wild animals in a zoo.

As we drove through the bush the vehicle hit a muddy ditch and got bogged down. No amount of revving or manoeuvring would budge it. The hunter got out to assess the situation and at the same time, a leopard appeared from behind the bush on my side of the vehicle. My mouth went dry with fear as it walked towards the driver. He managed to grab his gun and shoot it. But he only succeeded in wounding it and when he tried to shoot again all his ammunition fell out of his gun. He shouted for someone to bring a knife from the back of the land rover. In the meantime, the leopard attacked the hunter who was trying to stun the animal with the butt of his gun. After a frantic search we found one and Norman Salvage, who was sitting in the front ran to his aid. By this time, the leopard was standing on its hind legs and mauling the hunter. Norman managed to get behind the animal and stabbed it in the back. The knife must have penetrated the heart as the animal released its grip and fell to the ground dead.

The rest of us jumped out of the land rover and carried the injured man back to the vehicle. He was in a severe state of shock with bites to his hand and leg, he could hardly speak. We made him as comfortable as possible in the back of the Land Rover.

Norman and Andy managed to free the vehicle from the ditch. We then hurried back to Morogoro where the hunter was admitted to the hospital. As for us we returned home in a very sombre mood. There was little to be said after such a dramatic day.

We heard later that the hunter made a good recovery from his injuries, he was a very lucky man to have escaped with his life.

Several years later I happened to meet Norman again in South Africa. We chatted at length about the episode but he was very modest about his heroic act. I have to say that although this event took place almost fifty years ago, I can still recall quite clearly all the details of that fateful day.

Luckily I never experienced another episode quite like that in all my years in Africa. Norman is now retired in the UK."

During l956/7 we met a couple who had recently arrived from Rhodesia. He found a job in Motor Mart in the second-hand car sales department. Full of charisma, party-going and lavish in his tastes he was extravagant when throwing parties at his residence. I mean, a cinema screen with sixteen millimeter projector with shows for the children; a lamb on-the-spit, unlimited liquor, a blaring hi-fi and temporary wooden dance-floor all in the garden of his house. Coloured lights all illuminating the garden where everything took place, silhouetted with tall graceful palm trees and an expansive starry sky.

These parties were not in celebration of some special event but unusually frequent and we wondered how they could afford it. During the course of a conversation I had with him he explained that he and his wife had been divorced, not once, but twice, having been married originally and then re-married between the two divorces. This he explained to me prevented them by law from marrying a third time. Extraordinary. His spare time was spent building a racing car and it looked to my eyes to be a very professional job. He explained that he had done a lot of successful car racing in Rhodesia. I have no idea why he was building this racer in Dar es Salaam as, at that time there was no motor club of any sort, let alone a race track!

As time moved on, actually only a short period of time of probably less than fifteen months, Motor Mart discovered that they were twenty-two cars short in their stock!!

A court-case was held and instead of racing his car on a race-track, he ended up driving a tractor in Kingolwere Prison in Morogoro for five years.

Let us move on to another character in the person of **Wing Commander Francombe.** He was a pilot in the RAF during world war two and during that time had visited East Africa. His visit made him decide where to retire after the war. He bought a small *shamba* in Kenya but soon found that he missed the flying. Undaunted, he set about building a glider which he later flew successfully but, being a glider, restricted his sphere of activity. Determined to be able to fly to all parts of East Africa, he mounted a VW engine on top of the fuselage, just behind the pilot's seat and took off. Unfortunately this arrangement upset the balance and ability of the aircraft to fly and he crashed, necessitating a prolonged stay in hospital. Lying in bed he set about re-designing the plane and immediately after discharge, commenced the construction of his new venture. It had bigger wings and was therefore able to carry him and the engine into the air and fly very well except that no great height was able to be achieved.

The VW engine must have been rather second-hand because on his trips from Nairobi to Mombasa and vice-versa, the spark plugs would frequently oil up and he would land on the main road and clean the plugs and then take off and continue his trip. This could sometimes happen twice and he would therefore take almost a day for the single journey.

The plane, of course, was banned from using any of the commercial or air force airports so he had to navigate from private air fields to go from place to place. His normal method of navigating was following the road routes. Due to the very slow speed of landing and take-off and the short run required, the roads presented him with unlimited landing strips; provided the traffic was not too heavy.

When I say he was banned from main airports, he was actually permitted and asked to fly at an air-show at Wilson Aerodrome just outside Nairobi where we all saw him fly this extraordinary plane. It was similar to a glider but a little bigger, with an open cockpit right up in the nose and with the VW engine mounted above and behind his seat. The pilot sat with head and shoulders exposed. There was a particularly strong wind blowing and Wing Commander Francombe took off and circled the aerodrome twice and then came down very low, only about twenty feet off the ground and flew past in front of us spectators, against the wind. Well, the plane was so slow whilst against the strong wind and him purposely doing a slow run that I think a man running could almost have kept up with it. Flying so slowly we could see him with leather headdress and goggles and he looked like something out of the First World War, but soon he speeded up the engine and gained speed and then climbed higher and higher into the distance and towards his *shamba* somewhere near Mount Kenya.

During a business trip to one of our shops I was travelling on the Nairobi – Mombasa road and stopped at a small place called Simba for the night. Simba is an oasis on that dusty dry road as there is abundant water and one of our very great white hunters built a small thatched-roof hotel and retired there. Name – **J.A. Hunter**. He wrote a famous book just called *Hunter*. All of us read it and what a character-full life he led in the bush.

Latterly he joined the bandwagon of hunting safari organizers and leader of his own hunting safari business taking parties of foreign visitors out to hunt for trophies. His book is a must for anyone interested in East African hunting life, and what a sense of humour!

Having had a bath, I retired to the bar, (Cynthia would say "what else") before dining. It was a tiny bar only able to accommodate four or five at the bar counter and perhaps six drinkers sitting at two or three tables. Having ordered a beer I spotted an elderly gentleman entering at a shuffling pace who made straight for a bar-stool especially reserved for him and right next to the bar stool on which I was sitting. It was J.A. Hunter. A ready-prepared pipe and matches were lying on the counter in front of his stool and he picked these up, lighted and puffed while one of the two barmen, one white and one black, hastily poured a beer for him without being told what to do. He sucked at his pipe a few times then took a large mouthful of beer and slowly turned and looked around at the imbibers. Having seen nobody he knew he looked at me through his very old – glazed eyes and asked me who I was. After this his aged voice let me know who he was and then his mind wandered a little as we conversed very slowly and every three or four minutes he would put his pipe down and almost immediately lose sight of it and blame the barman for taking it away. It would be pointed out to him again and he would lift it to his mouth, suck and then blame the barman for removing the matches until they were pointed out to him lying underneath his hand. It was a slow conversation with a man who had become a legend in East Africa and I felt privileged to have had a half hour with the great man. He then went to dine.

In came a man who looked like Tarzan out of the movies. I do not exaggerate, big, young, handsome and very powerfully built and with an air of confidence but not over-bearingly so. He sat down next to me and we chatted over a couple of drinks. He was **Barry Chappel**, game expert, extreme game enthusiast and had been employed by the Game Department to stop the poaching of rhino in the area. A man full of 'zest for life' who had come out from the UK only very recently.

We dined together and he invited me to his residence which was only a few hundred yards away, in the bush. It was a *mtu* -built log cabin with a long drop a few yards away to the side. His furniture was two wooden soap-boxes and a cheap bed. One box to sit on and the other for his food supplies. He sat on the box and I on the bed. We chatted over a few whiskys, a bottle of which he had in his supplies. His story was absolutely fascinating. He lived there on his own and had a staff of four game scouts who were really observers and reported all the activity of any poachers in the area. When the latter were seen or suspected he would go out on foot as he had not been allocated a vehicle, and with the aid of one or two of his scouts, would pursue and arrest the criminals who were normally in the employ of the Indian duka-wallahs. As he did not drink a lot and had no vehicle he was supremely fit and looked it. I asked him how he would tackle the problem of a poacher running away, when spotted and he said that he had not encountered a poacher who could outrun him and that after a short distance they would normally tire and slow down and surrender. On a very few occasions he did have to rugger-tackle but he hated this as these citizens, he claimed, smelled far worse than any hyena.

The most effective way to success when dealing with these poachers was surprise and ambush.

Two years later I read a newspaper report of an accident to a Game Department Ranger who had been killed when the plane he was flying crashed and burst into flames. The name of the Game Ranger was Barry Chappel.

A Game Department friend of mine who later became a very great hunting friend described the accident. Apparently Barry had been having great success in the anti-poaching campaign and had asked for a light-aircraft to expand his sphere of operation as poaching was becoming more and more rampant due to the profits made by the *duka* owners and their compatriots. The department had put him through a pilot's course and allocated a light manoeuvrable aircraft to him. He was therefore responsible for a vastly expanded area around Simba with a bigger staff and organization.

He had spotted a large gang of poachers and was circling them. He had one passenger who was employed by the Game Department as his assistant. I gathered that he did not have a great number of flying hours and therefore was not a pilot of any substantial experience. During a sighting he was circling a gang and directing the ground staff towards this squad of criminals. Flying in ever-tightening circles and at too slow a speed, the plane stalled and plunged to the earth and to make matters worse, burst into flames. By the time rescuers arrived, Barry was severely burnt and died on the way to, or soon after admission to hospital. His passenger did not survive. I felt privileged to have known him for only a very short while and was shaken by the news.

Characters? They were all over the country and one only heard about or read of the great ones like the prominent settlers such as Delamere and members of the Government hierarchy. East Africa seemed to engender an atmosphere which brought out the 'characters' like moths to a candle. The country swarmed with them and one did not consider it unusal to continue to contact or hear of their exploits. Yes, we had some hilarious and dubious ones too. My mind now turns to one I remember and his name was **Paddy**. I shall not mention his surname as this story, although absolutely accurate might generate laughable dissention.

Our likeable friend Paddy had been a waiter in the NAAFI on an RAF Station during the war in the UK. As a waiter he was in a position to assimilate many many stories of those pilots who had just returned from sorties. He must have had a particularly retentive memory as was proved later. His ability to emulate the RAF jargon and stories was a branch of Walter Mitty's world in real life. He was very careful to keep his stories restricted in the face of his friends but if his audience was strange to him, he would immediately mimic the RAF vocabulary in an upper-class accent and regale them with his flying exploits during the bombing of Germany. All was very realistic and he could put these anecdotes across with such aplomb that his listeners were always impressed. His pals knew all about this and teased him mercilessly. His real-life job was that of a junior public servant but this was not nearly glamorous enough for his imagination.

He bought a new car. At the end of his tour he was given six months' leave, as was the usual government holiday before returning and he decided to spend his leave, instead of going back home, travelling in his new car with family to South

Africa and back. All went well and as an active Round Table member, he visited one or two members' meetings during his vacation. Paddy returned with big smiles and rejuvenated energy as we all did after 'long-leave'. After a short while he attended a meeting of the Round Table but in the interim a letter had been received by the Dar es Salaam Round Table from their associates in Salisbury in Rhodesia thanking the Dar Round Table for very kindly directing Wing Commander Paddy to the Salisbury meeting where they had been privileged to have his company and listen to the admirable exploits carried out by his squadron during the war! Well, Paddy had obviously achieved his ambition of basking in the glory of the reception given him in Salisbury and I doubt if he ever imagined that the Round Table in Rhodesia would inadvertently spill the beans!

The letter was received with loud and tolerant amusement and earned him the nick-name of 'Wing-Co'. I just do not know what the reply to Salisbury would have been.

In 1958, my company transferred me to Nairobi and, having had eight years of coastal humidity and heat, Cynthia and I were looking forward very much to the cool champagne air of five thousand feet in Kenya. We loved Dar es Salaam with the easy-going life and the beaches, the warm sea and the very, very likeable coastal Swahili tribes, our light clothes and our early meeting; marriage and the arrival of the two boys into our family.

Memories of Tanganyika

Before embarking on writing about our journey to Nairobi, I would like to dwell on the absolutely magnificent country of Tanganyika. It is a country of many contrasts and with the additional advantage, at that time, of the vastness and intensity of the animal hordes; was truly a marvellous place for any mortal being to live in and enjoy, especially for a young man.

Times may have changed and all the colonial values have been undermined and ridiculed, the indigenous people are now ruling themselves, but the physiognomy and geography of the country is still as magnificent as ever. Tanganyika; I still enjoy using this name instead of the modern nomenclature of Tanzania; has an immense variety of rich geographical features as have a large number of African countries south of the Sahara. Well, so many of the countries surrounding Tanganyika also have beauty and magnificence but I would like to extol the great virtues of the country in which we Tanganyikans (yes, let us call ourselves that if we lived and enjoyed the time that we dwelled and worked there) spent a large portion of our lives. What do we have? I could go on forever from one varying region to another and fill a few books which would all be very interesting but let me abbreviate and describe as much as possible on the limited paper I have.

The Government divided the Territory into Provinces – Southern, Central, etcetera but I will merely write about the regions and places I knew.

Our coast – beautiful sandy white beaches all with a coral reef and a myriad of small islands – absolutely hundreds of them, all coral. Water; warm all year round and because of the coral reef no shark attacks to the swimmers. Our two boys, Graham and John, learnt to swim – not in a swimming pool but in the sea. At high tide and near it, the water was calm and clear. Ideal in which to teach youngsters to swim. Due to the heat and the rapid evaporation the salt content was high and consequently buoyancy greater. These gorgeous beaches stretch for four hundred miles from the Macambique border on the Ruvuma River mouth to just south of Shimoni (on the Tanganyika/Kenya border) which is only thirty four miles south of Mombasa.

Of course the whole stretch of beach on our coast from north to south was lined with palm trees which were so plentiful that from the air they appeared to be almost like a great green carpet border. This border of palms had a width of, from the water's edge at high tide to perhaps about fifty yards inland. Opposite the Rufiji River mouth, where 'Rufiji', mentioned earlier, lived, is the beautiful island of Mafia only twenty miles from the shore. You could call it a smaller sister of Zanzibar, with no Arabs but a substantial boat-building industry. I visited it a number of times on flights to and from Lindi and Dar es Salaam. The vegetation was very thick, green and partly matted jungle. The big-game fishing all along this coast is much sought-after by wealthy fishermen from all over the world today.

In the south of Tanganyika there exists a colossal plateau of hot dense jungle in places and very heavily forested, stretching north from the Mocambque border for a distance of perhaps one hundred miles to the vast Selous Game Reserve, the biggest game reserve in the world. The road through this vast area commenced near Mbeya at Njombe after dropping down the escarpment and continued through Songea and Tunduru through Masasi and Newala to Lindi and Mtwara – a distance of some four hundred and twenty one miles (six hundred and seventy three kilometers) and in fact about as long as the whole Tanganyika coastline.

Let me digress for a moment; my first trip on this route took place in l956 and my position in the company was that of Shop Manager at Dar es Salaam but this also meant that at least once a year I was to travel through all the territory south of Arusha and missing Mwanza, to visit the agents selling our sewing machines. It would take me at least three safaris to cover this area each year and Zanzibar was also included.

These journeys were most enjoyable and unexpected events took place daily. Perhaps a flooded river-crossing impassable or a breakdown to our vehicle, (broken springs were common), road too muddy to traverse, bridge washed away, tyre failure, sickness to our crew of three – i.e. a mechanic, a salesman and myself, collision with animal, unexpected hailstorms or road washed away.

The four hundred and twenty one miles through the route mentioned earlier was, for the whole distance just soft sand surface. The P.W.D. (public works department) could not afford to put gravel down on a stretch of road of that distance so it amounted to a sand-track really. The bridges over the streams were totally inadequate and although we travelled in the dry season after the rains in May, most of them were in bad repair and had to be by-passed through the dry stream bed in preference to risking a collapse or just because the bridge was partially or totally washed away. It was rumoured that the P.W.D. builders would build the bridges with inadequate cement in the mix because they sold part of the allocation of cement to the *duka wallahs* and built the bridges with a weak mixture.

However, the aforementioned bothers were minor in comparison with one over-riding and unusual characteristic of this road of four hundred and twenty one miles. The sand surface formed into corrugations the like of which I have never encountered on all the bad surfaces which existed on our East African roads. These sand corrugations were wider spaced undulations and higher on the apexes and lower in the valleys than any other corrugations I have encountered anywhere. One would travel at a ridiculously slow pace at first as it seemed to be impossible to speed up without the vehicle tyres starting to fly from one apex of the corrugation to the other and thereby setting up a hazardous motion of the vehicle which became very difficult to control with any margin of safety. Of course, one travelled for an hour or two at low speed and then from frustration, increased pace, started flying, cursed and slowed down. Sometimes in sheer vexation I would put foot down and experiment with some high-speed bursts to see if I could skim along the tops if I went fast enough but after a few perilous exploits, prudence would prevail and we would settle down to a more sober slow grinding pace. After hour after hour of this bone-shaking with the dust piling thicker and thicker on our bodies, a break would be taken and we would stretch our legs and ease our aching limbs with a short stroll round the van. Within a few hours of our travel no colourbar existed between us three as we were all red! This was due to the poor dustproofing on the back doors of the gharries of that time and consequently the whole wagon became a vacuum cleaner. I was instrumental in our company importing especially, two American International three-quarter ton vans. International Motor Mart assured us that these very expensive vehicles would be able to withstand the rigours of Tanganyika roads but I am afraid their boast did not hold water. Our roads destroyed them and they fell to pieces like every other make of vehicle in Tanganyika. Those East Africans who lived there at the same time as I did will remember the saying that "one had to be careful to keep an eye open for the pothole that was often so big that it could hide an oncoming car" – slightly exaggerated but it gave a warning which was almost appropriate.

After digressing; back to the country terrain again. Central Tanganyika from North to South had a plateau which was at an altitude of between two and a half thousand and four and a half thousand feet. This area stretched from Serengeti in the North through Kigoma in the West to Mbeya in the South to Iringa and then back to Dodoma in the centre East. A vast, vast area in which the climate and seasons are totally salubrious. Brisk invigorating mornings and cool evenings with a mild warm temperature in-between. Cool-to-cold nights. No great differential between the cool and hot seasons, perhaps eight to ten degrees Celsius. I have given a very brief description of the largest areas of Tanganyika and now let's finalize with the remaining features of this magnificent country. The mountains and lakes.

One of the greatest mountains of the world, Kilimanjaro, majestically rises from the vast plains covered with game of every sort, large and small, visible for a hundred miles distant, capped with a large perimeter of snow all the year round rising to nineteen thousand feet. From every view round the mountain it is always an awesome sight and when flying over in a Dakota at a few feet above the crater rim, looking down is a sight one never forgets. I did it three times. The pilots of East African Airways would only do this if thepeak was clear of cloud but most tragically the fatal crash of a Dakota carrying a full load of passengers occurred in the

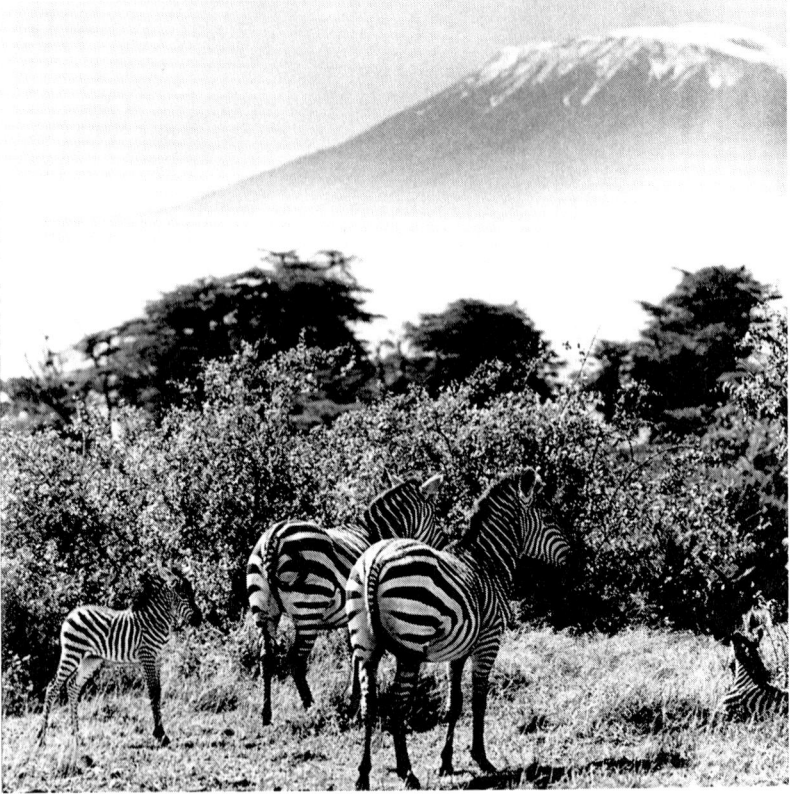

Mount Kilimanjaro

mid 195Os when the plane flew headlong into the mountainside (in cloudy weather) which resulted in a ban being put on pilots flying over instead of round Kilimanjaro. A friend of mine, the EAA Airport Manager of Dar es Salaam – 'Shubee' Schubert was amongst those who lost their lives.

Cheek-by-jowl next to Kilimanajaro but with a stretched deep saddle dipping in between is Mount Meru of twelve thousand, five hundred and seventeen feet, a small sister but nevertheless of imposing size and appearance. Tanganyika was lost by the Germans during the first World War and Britain therefore gained possession of the whole of this beautiful country.

There are many, many lower mountains such as the Usambaras at Lushoto, the Ulugurus near Morogoro, the mountains surrounding Mbeya and others.

In addition to the Selous National Game Reserve, Tanganyika has the famous world renowned Serengeti National Park and it is not for me to enthuse about this vast game sanctuary as it has been made well known to the world comprehensively and is truly one of God's great gifts to this planet.

Shall we move on to the lakes of Tanganyika? Look at four great and beautiful lakes, three of them being the greatest lakes in Africa – Victoria, Tanganyika and Nyasa. The other being Rukwa. Rukwa is totally within Tanganyika and the other three are so large that they are shared by no fewer than eight other countries. If we compare the sea coastline of Tanganyika with the lakes' waterlines in terms of length, we see that the coastline is only four hundred miles, as mentioned earlier, compared with nine hundred and twenty six miles of lakeside waterlines. All of these lakes are abundantly crowded with fish of all shapes and sizes and a great source of protein for all the inhabitants living close to the water. Lake Rukwa was alive with crocodiles and hunters would find it profitable to exploit this lake at a time when crocodile skins became fashionable for ladies' handbags, shoes, belts, etcetera. The population of crocs declined so rapidly that the Government was obliged to curtail the numbers of these reptiles being killed in order to protect the species and thereby keep the ecology of the area in balance. Lake Rukwa is close to the village of Lupa where, as I mentioned earlier, there had been a gold-rush and old Pop Wright was one of those embroiled in that jamboree. Most of the gold-diggers/panners did not make a significant find so the whole enterprise gradually fizzled out.

Eight years in a beautiful country as I have described is a bonus in one's life and we still look back on that time as some of the best years that we have enjoyed.

Having settled into our house over a period of four years and carried out a number of structural alterations to give us an extra room, large French doors from the lounge onto a patio with a pergola over it, meant that the upheaval of transferring to Nairobi was traumatic; but the thought of the champagne air and the excitement of a new venue, compensated for this. I decided that it would be more profitable to keep the property, rent it out and thereby enjoy the appreciation in value. It was one of the best investments I ever made. Selling the house in 1968 and then leaving East Africa enabled us to re-establish ourselves in a new country.

At this stage, I was not entitled to a private company car but only the use of a Singer van to and from work. I decided to send our furniture by a furniture removal company from Dar es Salaam to Nairobi. I did have a private car but thought it best to sell it before proceeding to Kenya, and buy another there. We now had two children – Graham and John, so as a family of four, our personal baggage was quite formidable. To save money for the Company and to make the journey a mixture of business and pleasure, we decided to travel by sea from Dar es Salaam to Mombasa and then by the famous night train from Mombasa to Nairobi. It cost less than travelling by air, with all our baggage.

KENYA

6

Kenya

We boarded a Lloyd Triestino ship, name forgotten and embarked at noon. There was no wharf big enough to berth a large passenger liner in Dar es Salaam harbour. We went through customs and then a small ferry-boat to the ship. If the ship did not berth but remained surrounded by water, even in a harbour, all goods and consumables were sold duty free on the ship. One paid for the voyage, which included meals but no alcohol. However, being duty-free, it was less than half the price of liquor ashore. I think I might have mentioned this before in my writing. We enjoyed the balmy weather while we sailed past innumerable islands after exiting Dar es Salaam harbour through waters in which I had goggled for eight years. The Lloyd Triestino ships always provided a tremendous evening menu and we enjoyed it to the full whilst the boys had been put to bed, after their separate children's meal in their dining-room. The weather I recall, was particularly calm. We had a nightcap on deck under the stars and then retired. The following morning I awoke early and discovered a fisherman trailing a long line over the rear deck. He was a crew member and had caught two fair-sized five-to-six pound barracuda. He complained that the Captain was travelling too fast to make up time and this had reduced his catch.

Approximately mid-day – our arrival at the beautiful port of Mombasa with that narrow entrance. We berthed alongside a big *godown* (warehouse) which housed offloaded passenger baggage, customs and immigration: this adjoined a larger *godown* into which we could see and that was jam-packed with incoming merchandise from cargo ships – bales, wooden boxes, heavy machinery, coils of rope, wooden barrels, foodstuff, tea chests, etc. The sweating bodies with upper torsos bare, struggling to lift, move, roll, push this merchandise were everywhere. Chaos reigned, voices of African and Indian supervisors were raised louder and louder in the humid atmosphere. Amid this pandemonium – it all worked; as our import and export business thrived through the years of colonialism and was forever on the increase as the farmers and small industries, cottage industries and small businesses increased their output.

Identifying and collecting our baggage in this heat was hot work as naturally, in those days, air-conditioning was virtually non-existent. But we were young and Cynthia looked after and generally kept the two boys under her wing while I engaged a porter, waded through the ships' luggage which had been offloaded from the hold by a crane with netfuls of passengers' cases, trunks and miscellaneous baggage on to the wharf-side, then trundled by man-pushed trolleys into our *godown*. Then through Immigration and Customs keeping a watchful eye to ensure that none of our boxes or trunks fell off the trolley and vanished without explanation. A *tekesee* (taxi) took us to the railway station and we later boarded the train leaving that evening for Nairobi.

Now, this train journey is one of the more unique experiences which we all, at one time or another, enjoyed. I shall come to the part of this journey later when I will give my impression of something unparalleled elsewhere in the world.

East African Railways was superbly run in the l95Os and 6Os. The trains were, as a rule, on time and the carriages were compartmented with totally clean sleeping arrangements. The compartments were spring-cleaned before each journey to Nairobi and vice-versa. There was heating, for the colder part of the journey during the night and early morning and especially at the higher altitudes as the trains neared and left Nairobi. All sheets and pillows were laundered and produced for sleeping in immaculate white condition; the blankets were also in new condition. A washbasin with running water – hot and cold, was situated in each compartment together with a fold-up table. Most compartments were four-berth and a few had two berths. The service to these compartments was especially efficient and a smartly uniformed steward would regularly proceed down the corridor playing a small xylophone or dinner gong just before a meal was to be served and enquire if passengers would need blankets and sheets for the night, hand out menus for the evening meal and enquire if any drinks should be served. He also arranged the seating in the dining-car if passengers required their meals there. If a meal was to be taken in the compartment he would discuss the menu with the passengers concerned and then at dinner-time, provide the passengers' requirements, all piping hot, in their compartment. After the evening meal or during it if the passenger would be eating in the dining car, the steward would enter the compartment, pull down the higher bunks and prepare the beds.

Well, as I said before, we boarded the train and the steam-engine pulling us chugged over the hills which surround Mombasa. After these hills had been negotiated it gained a little speed but it was a slow train – not even much speed at full-tilt with the wind behind. We ate in the dining car and the menu was sumptuous with expensive wines and champagne available but of which we did not partake. Soft drinks for the children and Cynthia and a beer for me. The boys were absolutely delighted as they had never been in a train before. After dinner straight into our pyjamas with bunks all ready prepared for us. The two boys were far too excited to go to sleep in a hurry.

At dawn the steward awakened us with his xylophone playing reveille as he walked along the corridor.

We now come to the exciting and unique experience of this journey. On a crisp and dry, clear morning as is the norm in the higher altitudes of Kenya, we washed and dressed and proceeded to breakfast in the dining car. The dining car had very large windows so that a great panorama of Africa was the view as we settled down to eat at table. We would probably be approaching the Athi Plains at this stage. We looked at the menu and ordered a splendid English breakfast with all the courses expected in an expensive hotel.

All this would be fairly normal in a top European Express train, but as we started crossing the Athi Plains, a sight met us through these panoramic windows (whilst we were sitting eating our breakfast) which was unparalleled throughout the world. Grazing very near the rail track were vast herds of animals of all the lovely species which inhabited the plains; zebra, wildebeest, kongoni, impalas, giraffe and a few Tommies and Grants gazelle, warthogs and many many ostriches. This great spectacle was taking place right under our noses as we glided along these great plains. What is more, the animals were totally unperturbed, either grazing, youngsters cavorting, or just staring at the train without any fear, all this beauty in the crisp clear air with bright blue skies and Kenya's champagne air of five thousand feet.

A marvellous introduction to our life in Kenya.

We were met at Nairobi Railway Station by Gordon Maugham who was to be my direct senior for a few years. It was at the time of the ending of Mau Mau and Gordon had been a major in the British Army during the conflict and fallen in love with the country and also with Thelma Marshall who was the daughter of 'Hoppy' Marshall, the local hangman. Gordon married this very charming lady and they had one daughter. Thelma was the Nairobi hairdresser whose business was called *Thelma's.* Gordon was the controller in the field of the whole of Kenya's Singer business and I was to be the Shop Manager for the two large shops we had in Nairobi, one in Hardinge Street opposite the New Stanley hotel and the other in Duke Street near River Road. This latter outlet was not only our 'downtown' shop but also our *godown* which held all the stocks for Kenya. I enjoyed the new challenge and went into it with the gusto which this climate induced.

Singers did not supply staff with living accommodation so we always rented and the Company contributed towards the rent. Our first abode was in Kikuyu which was really out in the sticks but even higher in altitude than Nairobi and cooler. Housing was very difficult to find but we did not want to stay that far out of Nairobi. The house was lovely and spacious but having been vacant for some time, was infested with fleas. What an ordeal! After a year we found an abode in Davidson Road near Westlands Corner. That was in l959. We overlooked the Nairobi River.

During the Mau Mau, firearms were at a premium. There were no strict rules on gun security until owners were being killed by the Mau Mau in the act of stealing their weapons. All gun owners were then forced to build fire-proof and thief-proof safes, and required to surrender their weapons to the police until such time as their safekeeping facilities were built into their houses, later to be inspected by the police firearms bureau and then approved. Coming from Tanganyika where we just stored them in a cupboard, I was required to hand in my two guns to the police until my safe was built. Gerry Pershouse, my very good friend from my bachelor days in Dar es Salaam had been transferred to Nairobi prior to me and he was at that stage the Assistant Engineer at East African Breweries. He sliced off the end of an oxygen cylinder and very expertly inserted a Chubb lock with five levers which was the lock demanded by the police. I then lay the cylinder down horizontally on the floor on two bricks in our main bedroom cupboard and poured concrete over it and shaped it into a rectangular oblong shape with the door and lock at one end. I have always thought what an excellent precaution this was that was enforced by the police and have always stored my firearms in that fashion ever since then.

Although Tanganyika was a great place to hunt game, Kenya game was far more accessible, and from Nairobi in particular; this was mainly due to the long distances one had to travel when living in Dar es Salaam. All the game hunting blocks were within easy reach of Nairobi – what a pleasure! Gerry now showed an interest in hunting and was addicted to the bush as was I. He was also an excellent cook which I am not. In fact it always amazed Cynthia that whenever I went out on a hunting safari my fare consisted of bread, margarine, tins of bully beef (corned Fray Bentos the best), coffee, condensed milk and a crate of beer. Oh yes – a can of drinking water as well if I remembered. With these ingredients I was able to keep going indefinitely without having to cook.

With Gerry on board, it was altogether different as he would not move into the bush without a comprehensive range of ingredients which would enable us to have at least one, but if breakfast is included, two hot meals a day. He, together with Jonathan Havelock was with me camping and hunting at the suspension bridge on the Tana River on one occasion and we had camped quite by coincidence right next to a fairly large anthill. The first thing Gerry did when he saw this anthill was to go out and shoot two guinea-fowl . He then dug a hole about two feet square into the side of the anthill, built a fire in the hole and after removing the innards from the guinea-fowl but with feathers still on, placed the birds into the heated hole after dousing the flames. He then closed the whole lot up with earth. An hour or so later, he took out these dusty looking birds, shook the earth off and gave them a bit of a wipe with a damp cloth. Whilst he was doing this the feathers and skin just dropped off, leaving a perfectly roasted and cooked meal which was divine tasting together with accompanying hot potatoes, yes, and gravy as well. You might call it 'bush luxury'.

That was not the end of it. I shot an impala for the pot to feed ourselves, our tracker and a few 'hangers on' who were doing odd jobs for us and what did Gerry do? He cut portions of meat into strips about eight inches in length, half an inch wide and about two inches across. He then made some magical marinade with plenty of pepper and a good dosage of salt plus various ketchups etcetera and dunked it for a few days. We did not have a refrigerator. Then up went a line from one tree to another and he hung the strips by threading the line through a pierced hole at the end, sprinkled them with more pepper to deter flies and other flying nasties and after two to three days the venison dried and we had 'Gerry-made' *biltong*. Absolutely delicious.

When both Gerry and I were stationed in Dar es Salaam, prior to our transfers to Nairobi, we became very good friends and have remained so for over fifty years although he and Eulalie and their two sons, Jonathan and Anthony emigrated to America in the late seventies.

It was through Gerry that I was happily paid to drink beer. Yes, paid to drink it, for two or three years when we were in Dar es Salaam. Although the Breweries were unaware of it, we were not breaking any rules and hatched a plan which worked 'par excellence'. It functioned like this. All breweries' permanent staff were allocated a crate of Tusker beer per week – twelve quarts of it. I soon discovered that Gerry did not like beer. He, bless his heart, drank gin. The way was therefore wide open for a top-level agreement to be ratified by us two tycoons. He would give me his crate of beer weekly and I would provide a bottle of Gordon's gin weekly. I paid shillingi *kumi* (ten shillings) for the bottle of gin. Gerry did not want the empties and crate returned to him so I sold them to the *duka-wallah* for twelve shillings. This meant that I gained the princely sum of shillingi mbili (two shillings) for drinking twelve quarts of Tusker per week. What bliss! Of course I had rather a struggle wrapping myself around twelve quarts a week so we had an increasing number of friends. All thirsty.

It came as a shock and I was totally devastated when Gerry was transferred to Nairobi. Cynthia claims that I was in tears.

This of course is a gross exaggeration but she also asserts that I went into state of purdah and sulked for weeks.

The reader will have to bear with me as I seem to revert frequently to anecdotes which took place previously in Tanganyika. I will, however, try and keep things in a general sort of sequence.

Back to our life in Kenya. I was revelling in my job and enjoying being in the immediate proximity of our Head Office as this enabled any problems to be solved with a decision quickly instead of communicating from as far away as Dar es Salaam to Nairobi. Communications in the 1950s in a place like East Africa were so primitive that it was often quicker to fly or travel by car to the point of the problem than to use the telephone or telegram! As an example, when I was stationed in Kisumu, it was quicker for me to communicate with our Shop Manager in Eldoret if he had a problem by travelling the seventy-five miles by car. The telephones were continually out of order. A telegram would frequently take up to a week to arrive at Eldoret sent from Kisumu. It took me just over an hour and a half if the roads were not wet and no bridges down.

I will do my best to give a picture of our lives as we lived them during this colonial period in the beautiful city of Nairobi. Naturally, Nairobi was, in the minds of all East Africans, regarded as the Paris of East Africa and when anyone came in from the bush, celebrations would take place. Bachelors with girlfriends would crowd into the few nightclubs (Travellers and The Avenue Hotel etcetera), hotel bars and restaurants and let off steam before returning to their outposts.

When we moved to Nairobi we were most fortunate to have a number of friends who previously had been resident in Dar es Salaam and we therefore felt more at home with our good friends the Pershouses, O'Tooles, Mike Greenway and a few others living not far from us. Children were put into nursery schools and Cynthia found a job working as a secretary/ shorthand typist for the chemists, A.H. Wardle in Government Road.

My company had, after a short while, provided a car for me. I bought a small car for Cynthia to travel backwards and forwards to Wardles and the nursery school.

Long Leave

The usual contract between employers and employees, commercial and government, contained a clause in which leave was specified. Normally, two and a half months' paid leave with fare paid to Europe. This was known as 'home leave'. In addition to this, one was given two weeks 'local leave' annually. We would receive a lump sum and could choose our mode of travel – sea or air. It took two and a half days by air and three weeks by sea from UK or ten days from the Mediterranean if one traversed the continent by car, when returning to East Africa.

As my parents had not yet met Cynthia, I decided to make the trip to South Africa on my first long leave in 1956 with our first-born child, Graham, who was thirteen months old. We also wanted to show Graham to Cynthia's parents in UK so a double journey was decided with Cynthia and Graham proceeding a few months earlier to UK. I was to follow and spend three weeks in Ottery St Mary in Devon with my family and my parents-in-law.

I left by air from Dar es Salaam and to connect with the UK-bound plane, I had to spend the night in Nairobi. In the meantime, Singers had given me a big compliment by offering a paid trip to our factory in Glasgow. So this had to be fitted into our three weeks in UK. Hunting Clan Airline then left Nairobi with me aboard and the first stop was for refuelling at Juba. The plane was a Vickers Viking, two engines – carrying about thirty-five to forty passengers and could only manage a cruising ceiling of four to seven thousand feet which meant that we bumped along the whole journey over bush; many hours over the Sahara, the Mediterranean and then circumvented the Alps to destination UK.

Our second stop was an overnight stop at Wadi Halfa. An hour before landing at Wadi Halfa, our aircraft encountered a severe sand storm and it was amazing to see just a red blanket when looking out of the window. The pilot had been flying on a 'homing' beacon directed from Wadi Halfa and was therefore able to fly straight to the landing strip but he did have a problem and he told me about it later. He said that the storm was developing ahead of him at a progressively increasing rate and had we arrived twenty minutes later he would not have been able to land as visibility was nearing zero. In those days, (1956), the pilot had to have good runway vision in order to land the aircraft safely. He would have been obliged to miss Wadi Halfa and carry on to Lucknor which was close enough for the fuel required but some way off his normal route.

As we disembarked from the aircraft I felt a hot, hot breeze and thought that I must be feeling the heat of the engine as I walked past it. Not so. This was the Sahara and I was feeling the breeze coming from the hot sands around the airstrip. I mean airstrip – that is all it was, no buildings or shelter of any sort. Just a couple of ancient vehicles waiting to take us to our hotel. The bus which took us was a rickety old Bedford and the road just a sandy track of about three miles before reaching our accommodation. As the sandstorm was still raging everything was covered in a layer of red sand but it was not too unpleasant when once indoors, except for the heat, and as I have said before, air-conditioning in those days was a rarity, especially in this neck of the woods.

I ordered a beer, as did an acquaintance whom I had met on the aircraft. Could you believe it? The beer was warm almost to the point of being hot and it cost shillingi *tanu* (five shillings)!! An extortionate price and probably the most expensive beer I had ever bought. The room was primitive but bearable. The same description could be applied to the dinner that evening and the breakfast next morning.

The following day we took off and bumped across the Sahara at about four thousand feet. So low that we could feel the desert heat all the time. We could quite clearly see the occasional oasis but they were few and far between. Our view was sand and more sand and more sand. I might mention that the Vickers Viking had no cooling (air-conditioning) or pressurization. The time from Wadi Halfa to Bengazi was a number of hours, exactly I cannot remember but perhaps six or seven. I was lucky enough not to be sick but I would say that probably more than half of the passengers were resorting to paper bags for most of that leg of the trip.

Coming in to land at Bengazi in Libya I was interested to see two round bomb craters still existing in the sand and stone. One very deep and the other not so deep and I was told that these were part of the aftermath of the second world war.

After refuelling – out over the Mediterranean, it was much cooler and most interesting with its ships and blue water. It was a shorter flight to Malta and then into the Phoenicia hotel with sheer luxury abounding everywhere. The Queen and the Duke had spent part of their honeymoon there and so one can imagine how grand it was. My acquaintance and I wandered into that part of the town close to the hotel but not too far as we had been warned not to venture too far. The renowned GHATS area was not too far away and should be avoided as one could be mugged. Anyhow, the Phoenicia was palatial and beautiful and what a contrast from our East African hotels and the Wadi Halfa grotto.

We departed from Malta very early in the morning and then made one last refuelling stop at Nice and at the same time, were treated to a sumptuous breakfast in an hotel at the Nice Airport overlooking the Mediterranean.The last leg was flown over southern France and then over the sea – probably the Bay of Biscay, and then on to London, Gatwick, I think.

The complete journey from Dar es Salaam to London took just over three days and three nights and was a very interesting experience when compared with today's eight or nine hours seeing nothing but air and more air.

As I was born in South Africa and educated there, this was my first visit to the UK. When an early teenager I had spent two years with an elderly aunt (who taught me to sing) – she had studied music and graduated from the Royal Academy of Music spending two years in London, and a short time in Scotland. She had regaled me with fascinating stories of life in London and imbued an intense spirit of curiosity in me. I could not therefore, wait to see this great city and country which I had heard so much about. I was brought up to revere my ancestors and greatly admired my paternal grandfather who was born in Kelso in Scotland in l855 and sailed to South Africa in a sailing ship in l880 where he stayed for the rest of his life.

Well, here I was now about to accomplish one of my travel ambitions and it was a great feeling coming in low over the green English countryside before landing.

We travelled into London and then I left my erstwhile pal and taxied to London Paddington and boarded the train for Exeter, Devon where Cynthia was waiting for me with Graham, who was a year old. The train was an express stopping only at a few stations and marvellously modern (at that time) and yes, drawn by a steam engine. It was very fast but nevertheless I could clearly see the green, green sylvan countryside of England with all its streams, massive trees, beautiful fields with sheep and cattle grazing with rolling hills in the background. This was what I expected it to be like and I was thrilled to be here at last.

Cynthia, Graham my father and mother-in-law, with whom Cynthia was staying, were all there to meet me to take me to Ottery St Mary, close to Teignmouth where my in-laws had bought a temporary abode. It was on the outskirts of the village of Ottery St Mary and really rural, surrounded by fields next to a big farmhouse with all the sheds and barns which these English farms seem to have. We woke up to a view over green fields with hedges round them and cows and sheep peacefully grazing. The semi-detached house my Pa-in-law had purchased was a comfortable little house and I started to enjoy the luxury of being in England. One of the activities we enjoyed was walking in the farmer's field opposite, with his permission, collecting mushrooms. Lovely old pubs close by.

As I mentioned earlier, Singers had arranged a visit for me to our factory in Glasgow, Scotland and so, in order to see as much of the country as possible, I decided to buy a second-hand car and travel by road, stopping at small hotels on the way. To obtain a car, I scoured the second-hand car dealers in Exeter and found a 1946 Morris Ten which seemed in working condition. The dealer promised to buy it back from me after a month at the same price, less a very reasonable fee and so we agreed upon this: all verbal.

I took the car and as soon as I returned to Ottery, proceeded to wash and polish it. To my surprise, after I had removed the city grime by washing and polishing, underneath was a very nice shiny car and it drove very well with no ominous sounds from the engine. Everything, or almost everything of importance seemed to work, gears, brakes, steering etc. I think the amount I paid for it was fifty pounds and the dealer's fee - ten pounds. That included the licensing .

To acquire the feel of driving in England and to test the car, we drove to many parts of Devon and I was fascinated by all the lovely Devonshire country-side with its hills, coastline and greenery. Time flew and soon it was time for our journey to Scotland. We left Graham with his grandparents and travelled via the west side of England through Bristol,

Manchester, Dumfries to Glasgow. In l956 there was no MI so we drove through the villages, towns and big cities on comparatively narrow roads following road signs on a route which we had previously mapped out from our road map. It was surprisingly easy to follow the route as the road signs were all clearly marked. When I look back on that trip I think how much more pleasurable it was than belting up the MI from London to Scotland with all the traffic we have these days.

Our old Morris behaved very well and it took us two and a half to three days before we arrived and settled into the Ivanhoe Hotel in St Enock's Square in Glasgow, at the company's expense. I was given VIP treatment and was fetched by a chauffeur and driven the five miles to our Singer factory each day, for three days. A guide was given to me by the name of Mr Johnstone who was perhaps five feet six inches tall and with the noise of the factory machinery and his broad Scottish accent, I had to bend down and put my ear close to his voice. The whole experience of actually seeing the process of making thousands of sewing machines from the beginning, (casting the heads in colossal furnaces), to the finished product, was to stand me in very good stead in my later career in Singers. There were l,5OO workers and the factory was well spread out having six sections to see during the three days I was there. I might mention that I was given a sumptuous lunch each day in the directors' dining room and privileged to be seated next to the managing director who was a cigar-smoking American, (did not offer them around), and his heads of departments – twelve in all – at a table of such great length that it would surely have held twenty with ease. The managing director drove, of course, the latest Cadillac with left-hand drive.

We drove back to Devon but also visited Edinburgh on the way back locating the ancestral research offices there and obtaining as much information as possible about the name Trotter – you know – origin, location, history etc. I discovered that the origin dated as far back as 1050 when a person called Robert Trotter was tenant-in-chief of King Edward the Confessor. But that is another story and fairly lengthy so I will not go into it.

Return to East Africa.

Our journey down to Devon was uneventful and we only stayed there for another two weeks before boarding our plane to return to Dar es Salaam to immediately start our road journey to my parents in Natal in South Africa.

Whilst Cynthia had gone ahead of me to the UK, I had prepared my old 1941 Plymouth for the journey – decarb, new big-end bearings, shock absorbers, tyres, brakes and so forth and I felt confident the old girl would carry us the two thousand five hundred miles safely. It did. However, the roads were all very dusty as there was no tarmac in 1956 until we reached South Africa, but northern and southern Rhodesia did have 'strip roads' which was one step better than just plain murram and corrugations.

First stop Iringa, at the very pleasant Iringa Hotel in which I had previously stayed a number of times when on business. Cool, crisp air, no humidity at three thousand feet. Next to Mbeya, and into the Mbeya Hotel which I have described previously. At this stage I had discovered, to my dismay, that the old Plymouth had shocking dust-proofing. It was akin to a vacuum cleaner and I decided to stop early every day so that

The old vacuum cleaner

I could shovel (almost) all the dust out of it and prepare for the next day's journey. We therefore stopped at about five pm each day from then on which meant that our safari would take longer than anticipated. Next stop, over the border from Tanganyika to Northern Rhodesia to a place called Mpika. It was a few miles off the beaten track and totally in the bush but recommended to me before as a comfortable but primitive little central African-type inn. It turned out to be just that with about six rooms for guests, a bar, dining room, verandah, parking lot for cars and totally enclosed by thick bush. The proprietor and his wife ran the establishment with a staff of Africans and he was an interesting man of middle age with one leg missing from just above the knee. He had been an elephant hunter for ivory for many years.

Unfortunately for him, when close to a good sized tusker, his gun had misfired and the elephant had charged before he could reload. It gripped him with its trunk and tossed him up and away. He landed on the ground and was stunned and lying down. The elephant then went to him and stamped on and crushed his leg and foot, turning him over and over again with its tusks and trunk. He was extremely lucky that at that point the great beast must have assumed that he was dead and wandered off leaving him to crawl a short distance before his tracker located him, picked up him and his gun and helped him to hobble some miles back to his camp. He then had to drive his Land Rover to the nearest doctor and this was the most difficult part of the episode as he kept passing out. But he eventually arrived in civilization and was hospitalised. The leg could not be saved so they amputated.

That put an end to his ivory hunting after which he built and opened an hotel. All this was described to me over a beer in the bar during the evening by another inmate.

From Mpika to Mkushi River where we stayed at a delightful little hotel overlooking the Mkushi river falls and a lovely sound of the falls in our ears during the night. This, after days and days of dry dusty Tanganyika roads and then dusty strip roads in Northern Rhodesia. Let me describe the strip roads. They were strips of tar macadam about two feet wide, left and right with the strips at the right width to enable the driver to keep his two front tyres on the strips if he concentrated hard. There was not a great deal of traffic in those days but the main problem was what to do when oncoming cars approached. Who would give way? Both, of course, but now and again the oncoming driver would put his foot down and hog both strips so at the last few seconds the other driver would swerve off and curse the manners of these Rhodesians. As we were East Africans (and therefore superior to Rhodesians) our egos were somewhat dented by this ignoble behaviour.

After Mkushi River our next stop was Kafue. This was the first rough and ready hotel since our departure and right on the main north/south highway which ran straight through the centre of the town. After a badly cooked meal in the dining room Cynthia started to feel queasy, then found that she could not sleep. Shortly after entering her bed she was up and about; then throwing up and this then continued throughout the night. Fortunately our room was 'en suite'; she spent most of that night hanging her head over the toilet. In addition to her being sick, we had the noise of heavy trucks trundling past our abode with pop music hissing and wailing from some sort of night club directly opposite.

Next morning I sought help from the receptionist who dosed the patient with (an overdose) of entero-vioform. This was a normal medical concoction used by all of us in those days to counteract a stomach upset and was very effective but only with the correct number of drops. Well, she poured herself into the car as best she could. I settled Graham into his child car-seat which was between the driver and her. Within a few miles severe stomach pains set in and she was writhing in agony. We were approaching the Zambezi river at Beit Bridge when she asked me to find a doctor. The heat was becoming intolerable as we descended lower and lower into the Zambezi Valley where we discovered that the Rhodesians called this month (October I think it was) – suicide month – because of the heat. There was nothing but heat, dirt and bush; so where was I to find a doctor? I was so alarmed at her condition that when I saw a small track leading off to our left under a sign saying something like 'Factory Compound', I swung off and followed this track for about two miles before I came to what looked like labour lines. A few Africans were wandering around in the heat. My Swahili was greeted with blank incomprehension but driving around slowly I found something called 'Office'. I entered and explained the position. The office worker (only one in a fairly big room), gave me directions to their clinic where he could not guarantee that the clinic attendant would be 'in situ'. I was lucky – he was. I explained, once more, the situation and then brought my poor wife into this rather neat and tidy, but primitive surgery. The English-speaking medical attendant then said that when the labourers had a tummy-ache, he gave them a dessertspoonful of 'this medicine'. He held up a bottle with a white coloured fluid inside it. Well, anything is often better than nothing. I first looked at the label. It was 'Bismuth of Soda'. I asked him to administer 'this medicine', which he then did.

The thatched roof shade of the clinic was a relief from the heat. We sat her down and rested for about ten minutes. To our amazement there was an almost immediate improvement. When the pains started to recede she gave me permission to resume our journey and walked unsteadily to the car. I would say that within an hour her pain had vanished. We could then breathe a sigh of relief. God bless that angel in the bush or should I say, that black angel in the clinic.

We by-passed Salisbury and travelled through to Bulawayo where my sister lived with her family, and were received rapturously by them after our long journey.

The Hills family then took us around Bulawayo to the places of interest and one particularly pleasant memory to me was a picnic to the Matopos, so of course we visited Cecil Rhodes' grave. As Bulawayo is only a one-day journey by train to the Victoria Falls, we decided to leave Graham with Elaine (my sister) and her family then travel to see these great falls which we had not seen before. We booked in at the luxurious Victoria Falls Hotel and stayed there one day and two nights. In those days, one travelled from the hotel to the falls on a small trolley on rail tracks – owned by the hotel – only a distance of about three hundred yards and then walked fifty yards to the rain forest. The view from the rain forest of the falls was awe-inspiring, a sight one never forgets.

After the rain forest was the railway bridge which spans the Zambezi and also divides Northern and Southern Rhodesia. Once having seen that colossal cascade of water tumbling

Cynthia viewing the Victoria Falls

over the greatest falls in the world into that deep abyss below, one is humbled; it is a sight of such magnitude that one will just never forget. I failed to mention the noise – the great volume of water surging over and down, then crashing to the bottom produces a heavy ear-deafening rumble which makes it impossible to converse properly. One has to shout and scream into one another's ears to communicate at all.After returning from Victoria Falls to Bulawayo we continued south, soon crossing the border from Southern Rhodesia into South Africa. The old Plymouth had taken the roads very well but the water in the radiator was inclined to boil if I put my foot down too hard. This necessitated 'featherfoot' on the accelerator when on any incline. As a result, our progress was very sedate. But crossing the border into South Africa meant that we had tarmac thereafter. This gave us more confidence as the most arduous part of our journey was now behind us. No dust – just fresh air for the old vacuum cleaner to suck in.

It is interesting to note that after living in East Africa for five years, we were surprised to find no wild game whatsoever when travelling through Northern and Southern Rhodesia.

We arrived in Estcourt, Natal and travelled to my parents' farm to present my very new wife and child to my family. Only my sister in Bulawayo had met them and we did the rounds meeting all the other members of my family. This took place over the next few weeks of our remaining leave before embarking on a Union Castle ship (the *Rhodesia Castle*) leaving Durban harbour and sailing back to Dar es Salaam with our car, stopping at Lorenco Marques and Beira en route.

The long leave described above was not our normal route and on that occasion we fitted South Africa in especially for Cynthia to meet my family. Durban did not suit her at all as she suffered from asthma and became very ill there when staying with my brother George and his wife. The doctor advised us to steer clear of Durban and take her back to the clear crisp air of Estcourt, which we did and this cured her asthma during the rest of our stay in South Africa.

In the years that followed when I took long leave we always travelled to England by air and returned by sea either embarking at Tilbury in London or, travelling across the continent by car and embarking at Trieste in Italy. Latterly, when I had gained executive status in Singers, a new car was normally waiting for me upon arrival at London Heathrow and we had the pleasure of using this during our long leave. On one occasion when returning, we left Teignmouth in Devon, together with my parents-in-law and our two first-born (Graham and John). We travelled across the continent covering Belgium, Luxemburg, France, Germany and Austria where we stayed for a week. After leaving my in-laws in Austria to fly back to the United Kingdom on their own, we then travelled south through Italy and Trieste where we embarked on a Lloyd Triestino ship (the *Europa*) with our car to sail to Mombasa. Then finally, in our nice new *gharri* (Swahili for car) by road from Mombasa to Nairobi. It was a spacious Peugeot station wagon, well able to accommodate us four adults plus the two children on the continental stretch. It also had a large roof-rack where all our suitcases were stored. This was very necessary when carrying four adults and two children on a long journey.

7

People, places & hunting
in Kenya

It was always a pleasure to be back home among all our friends and familiar surroundings. East Africa really was our home. It also gave me a feeling of satisfaction to dive back into my work with renewed energy and take control again of the business for which I was responsible. I was very happy in my job. Like many of my compatriots I put every ounce of energy into it. People in the UK thought that we East Africans lived a life of luxury and exploited the natives. Nothing could be further from the truth. To run a business properly and to employ the indigenous people - and I had hundreds working under me - required an enormous amount of training time. This benefited them all. I found the *Kikuyu* eager, quick to learn and also very keen to get ahead. Of all the tribes with whom I worked in East Africa I found the *Kikuyu* to be the quickest on the uptake and the most intelligent.

The coastal Swahilis were of a very friendly and easy-going disposition; therefore they were the most pleasant of all the tribes. Always smiling and friendly, even under difficult conditions with set-backs of one sort or another. Unfortunately, malaria took its toll and they lived with it. They still do but it makes them lethargic - however, as I said before, they are a cheery lot under difficult circumstances.

The Lake Victoria tribes were lazy in the extreme (the Luo in particular) and *bilharzia* was their principal set-back. I was speaking to a doctor in the Kisii Hotel about bilharzia and he told me, with many medical terms which were over my head, that the tribes around Lake Victoria were ninety-nine percent affected by bilharzia and each man and woman lived with it normally until death. At the time of carrying out examinations during post mortems, he had removed from the spine, bilharzia worms (up to a full dozen) half-an-inch thick and these parasites were probably as old as the host – in other words, had lived in his/her spine throughout their lives. This, of course, retarded the growth of the person and made them very lethargic. It also ensured that the host never put on any weight.

Whilst dwelling on the subject of Kisii, I must mention that as late as the early 1960s trepanning was still being carried out by the local witch doctors. It was banned by the government but this did not deter the witch doctors or the brave patients. They must have been extraordinarily courageous to undergo the operation, just to get rid of a persistent headache. It was performed like this. If a patient suffered from an excruciatingly bad headache, he would consult the ubiquitous witchdoctor who would, for a fee, send the hapless patient to the operating 'surgeon'. A consultation would take place and if the patient was prepared to pay for the procedure which involved the services of the surgeon with two assistants (these two assistants had to be physically of good strong stature), then agreement would be reached. Later when all operating instruments had been prepared and the assistants duly instructed, action would commence. All such unnecessary things like hygiene were abandoned as the patient lay down on a large cowhide out in the open. The two strong young men then placed their strength and weight on the unfortunate patient's shoulders and arms and probably the head also. The surgeon had previously shaved the head.

He then proceeded to use a sharp razor-blade (forget anything as sophisticated as sterilization) to make two incisions about four to five inches in length from front to back on the apex of the skull. The depth of the cut was right to the skull bone. The two incisions were made about one and a half to two inches apart and a witchdoctor's brew was used as a sort of sort of ghastly paste to stem the blood-flow. After the skull was reached the skill of the surgeon was required to be at his delicate best to cut into the bone with a previously blunted razor-blade. It had to be previously blunted so that he could use a sort of sawing action and this, so it was said, allowed him to cut very delicately through the bone but no further so as to avoid damaging the brain. The two strong assistants would be doing sturdy work sweating away holding the patient as still as possible and probably tied a gag over his mouth to dampen as many unengaging sounds as possible. After the surgeon had completed sawing the length of the two grooves into the skull, he would then turn at right-angles and saw an incision at each end of the two lines to form a rectangle four to five inches long and two inches wide. This rectangle of skull bone would then be able to be lifted and removed. And removing it relieved the pressure on the brain!! Headache cured!! I never discovered how they completed the operation of sealing things off after all this procedure but I saw a photograph of the head of a successfully recuperated patient and it just left a flat shallow depression with no hair. This method of curing headaches was made illegal as the mortality rate was high. Oh yes, I forgot to mention that spectators were allowed, or automatically occurred as the whole thing was done out in the sunshine and the surgeons were at pains to demonstrate their prowess to all and sundry. The results − well, if the patient survived I don't think he dared admit to any further pains in his head in case further 'treatment' would be necessary.

Back to Nairobi. Mum (Cynthia) had been educated at the Kenya High School for Girls in Nairobi and before that at Kilimani and Parklands Primary schools and of course knew a number of ex school friends who lived there. The Kenya High School I might mention was affectionately known as the 'Heifer Boma'.

I had a few friends who had previously been transferred to Nairobi and therefore the move from Dar was a double bonus. My breweries' friend, Gerry Pershouse (whose bush culinary expertise was described earlier) was one of them and he was interested in hunting. I immediately contacted him with a view to future action. The fact that I had bought a good rifle in Dar es Salaam was an incentive for him to do the same. He bought a lighter rifle as he was not keen to go after big game.

Our first hunting safari together was to the suspension bridge on the Tana River at the foot of Mount Kenya. It was a most imposing sight to look up at the great snow-covered peak from our camp which was next to the river and about two hundred yards downstream from the suspension bridge. Being suspended from thick cables, it was one of the few suspension bridges I knew of in East Africa which was able to carry motor vehicles. A veritable haven surrounded us of miles and miles of bush teeming with all sorts of game. No human habitation at all. The presence of a camp being set up always attracted the attentions of the local tribe and after a day of settling ourselves in a most unlikely creature turned up and announced that he was a tracker. His name was

Daudi. He was from the Wanderobo tribe and consequently knew no Swahili, was as old as the hills with exceedingly bandy legs and only about four feet ten inches in height.

Daudi turned out to be the most accomplished tracker I ever had the pleasure of hunting with. He knew all the species in the area and where to locate the likes of waterbuck, kudu, all the gazelles and buffalo which were what I was after. When, after much sign language he had grasped which animal I was after we set off and he seemed to know every inch of the land and would set a merciless pace which was very difficult to keep up with even though I was young and very fit. His eyesight was able to pick up all the minutest pieces of evidence which allowed him to follow the game at a fast pace. His eyes looked old and worn but this was deceptive as those old peepers were able to pick up not only all signs necessary for an accurate following, but any animal at a great distance. Things like a broken stalk of grass, footprints fresh or old and there were normally dozens of different types of spoor imprints, dung (shape, texture, old or fresh and smell) animal body smell or hair left on tree-trunks, sounds, birds which alerted the game, direction of wind; all were signs which this man could assimilate simultaneously. The qualification which I gave him was *Master Tracker (Hons),* not acquired by studying text books and passing written examinations through school and university. He could not even read or write. No, his qualification was acquired by using his 'text books'. His text books and dictionary were the fauna and flora and the sylvan growth in which he had been brought up; two vast subjects. But let us not rhapsodise further on his accomplishments - let us get on with the hunting.

The main necessity to start off with was for the pot so he took me to a place close by where I shot an impala and this enabled me to test the accuracy of the rifle and most important – my eye. We had, of course, set up a target in camp and done a zeroing in. But the real thing is the best to finally test a rifle as it makes one feel more confident.

I was keen to get after the buffalo and therefore set off with just Daudi the following day. Gerry was not interested in going after big game and Jonathan Havelock, his step-brother and son of Sir Wilfred, was still a teenager who had just come to enjoy the camping and open air. Daudi set up a furious pace with bent back, bare feet, bandy legs and a half-crouch, all of which made me keep attempting to restrain his speed but to no avail. He, being so short and crouching, without the encumbrance of a rifle to carry, could negotiate thick bush much better than I, at almost double his height. In the 'old days' hunters would always employ a gun-bearer as their rifles were almost always big heavy hard-hitting double-barrelled 400s or 500s which weighed a ton in comparison with my .375 single barrel. I always carried my rifle; partly because I did not trust a gun-bearer to stand steadily and hand me the rifle if a big animal such as a buffalo ambushed us. I had heard many stories of gun-bearers taking off in reverse with the *bwana's* gun in hand! And the other reason was that my .375 was light enough for me to be able to move forward without undue hardship.

After about four or five miles Daudi reduced his savage pace enabling my somewhat bruised lungs to recover while he kept raising his head and looking forward. Very shortly he started a slow motion, tense attitude in his pace, staring ahead intently, then testing the wind every fifteen-or-so paces by lifting a pinch of sand and letting it drift down from his held-up hand thus showing the direction of the breeze. Within ten minutes of this careful stalking we sighted the buffalo. It was a massive herd of about four to five hundred animals silently grazing in the lush knee-height grass.

My hunting friend René Vidot, whom I mentioned earlier, had lectured me in the art of stalking animals. Take the elephant to start off with, he has poor eyesight but good hearing and a marvellous sense of smell. But normally he is making such a noise foraging, stripping trees and pulling branches that noise is not important when stalking. On the other hand, he would pick up a metallic sound, such as the click of any of the mechanisms of a rifle from a long way off even if the foraging and breaking sounds of his feeding were being made.

His lecture covered all animals such as lion, leopard, zebra, antelope, rhino and buffalo. When approaching animals such as buffalo, he said your movements should be extremely cautious, very slow. The buffalo has reasonable eyesight, the zebra has telescopic eyesight. The latter can pick up a movement or shape, hundreds of yards away and there is always a lookout who will immediately alert the herd if he is at all suspicious. Sound? Well René said that you must learn to move absolutely soundlessly. All things such as whispering (almost breathing) are forbidden. You should be so quiet whilst stalking that you would be able to hear a chameleon fart.

Daudi qualified with ease in all aspects of René's rules but I was still a novice and every footstep I put down sounded deafening to my ears. Heart-beat increasing, sweating more than usual in the heat.

We crept closer and closer and the bush and grass cover was becoming more sparse so we had to be doubly careful in our stalking; Daudi in front with me attempting to crouch as low as him. It was however, a long distance between ourselves and the quarry and Daudi, I could see, was worrying about the direction of the wind which seemed to be gusting a little.

Suddenly they became suspicious of our presence and stopped grazing and then peered in our direction. This they did for a period of perhaps one minute and this gave me a chance to slowly lift the .375 and aim. However the distance between them and me was a good one hundred and twenty yards and at that distance I was not really able to select a good killing position like, for instance, neck, shoulder etcetera, carrying a good pair of horns. However, being a novice I fired at the one nearest but did not hear the thud of the bullet striking and realized that a miss had almost certainly taken place.

The next thing that happened was a stampede.

There must have been about five hundred in the herd, in fact the largest herd I ever remember seeing. They did not realise exactly where we were and galloped in a direction which took them close by to us as they careered towards safety. Now, because they came past us at a distance of about fifty yards, the noise of the herd galloping was like an express train thundering along. Five hundred buffaloes equal two thousand hooves pounding the earth and I just stood there ogling the spectacle and listening to this great train of animals in a headlong rush.

Daudi was disgusted at my failure to find a target but said nothing. However, I could sense that he justifiably had derogatory thoughts about me and my rifle's ability.

I decided to investigate the point where my target had been and ensure that there was no blood spoor. There was not and this was not surprising to me although I was hoping for one.

We followed the direction in which the herd had travelled and whilst doing so I discovered another peculiarity of these animals. For perhaps a mile of following their spoor, which was easy, we were encountering lone bulls or cows which were hiding in clumps of thick bush and which would gallop off as soon as we were close. This made for some exciting moments when I expected a charge but luckily this never materialized and each and every one of them just galloped off after the herd which had travelled at speed and became way beyond our reach.

This taught me two good lessons. Not to shoot at too great a distance as this does not ensure that a good accurate shot is made. Number two is that the buffalo is to be regarded with great respect. The fact that they do not all join in the stampede and hide instead, whether from lack of inclination to run a distance, thrown out of the herd or in order to ambush the hunter or whatever, it means that one must keep one's wits ready to be prepared for the unexpected.

At the time that I was hunting (1950s and 1960s) the telescopic sight was being introduced and a few models were available to the marksman;   very expensive. There were many schools of thought on this – one propounded that this sight made for more accurate shooting and therefore caused less stress to the animal as a quick mortal shot could be achieved. I agreed entirely with this point of view but then the rifle being used would have to be high-powered with a greater flat trajectory if hunting big game. All rifles of this pattern were never of a large bore. All large bore rifles for hunting big game were made for stopping power at close range. So when hunting elephant, buffalo and rhino a large calibre rifle with a telescopic sight would be unnecessary due to the hunter being close to his quarry. There was no weapon of sufficiently large bore which could be used at a distance of more than forty or fifty yards due to the short flat trajectory of the bullet. I am thinking now of every weapon of more than .375 magnum up to .5OO.

These were the rifles being used and 'stopping power' on an animal charging at close distance was of paramount importance. Of no small significance was the fact that quick instinctive accurate shots could not be made at close quarters with a telescopic sight mounted on the top of the barrel. In these instances only one sight could be used and this was the old-fashioned V or U sight with a bead. I quote from *Safari*, the book written by Bartle Bull:

> "On subsequent safaris, Bell (Karamoja Bell), learned to value the qualities of the modern, high powered rifle: weight and accuracy. Its light weight enabled him to carry his own weapon all day, until it became an extension of his arm and he could raise and use it with effortless steadiness. To perfect the steadiness of his aim, Bell performed endless drills with his rifle extended in one hand. Soon he learned that a small bore rifle is reliable only with a brain shot, for the heart and lungs can absorb more punishment and

143

take longer to bring the body down. Carefully Bell learned the precise angles to the elephant's ten-pound brain, roughly the size of a loaf of bread. He used the ear root (hole) and the eye to plot the location of the brain".

Bell never used a telescopic sight: they had not been invented at that time. I never used a telescopic sight and agreed with most of my hunting friends that the telescopic sight gave the hunter an unfair advantage. Pure hunting to us was to stalk our quarry and then shoot accurately. Telescopic sights were best left to the wealthy clients of hunting safari businesses.

I have described previously how Gerry Pershouse with his expertise in cooking kept us very well fed on good food and I spent a number of safaris in this same location using the same camping spot which was so picturesque.

I must now relate how we attended to nature, which was of course the normal way of taking a spade and a roll of jazz paper, digging a hole and returning to camp after filling in the hole. This was fine and dandy but at night all sorts of animals came to the river to drink.

Gerry, unfortunately, found it necessary to perform at about nine o'clock one evening and proceeded to carry out the normal functions. It was dark but there was a moon. He did not take a torch with him. After about four or five minutes there was a wild scream and Gerry came running back to camp at speed – bereft of any garments from the waist downwards.

"Something moved in the bush right next to me" our hero exclaimed breathlessly. He grabbed his rifle, so did I and we stalked back with rifles at the ready – (him minus trousers), together with torches. As we approached the area of his action in the bush what did our torches pick up? A lovely water-buck. A doe staring at our torches with large inquisitive eyes and then her mate, not more than ten yards further on.

This incident provoked a huge number of ribald comments and laughter from Jonathan and me and our other friends when we returned to Nairobi. Gerry retrieved trousers and spade and the two lovely antelope delicately moved away.

More About Kenya

Although we did move an awful number of times during our stay of seventeen years, this was not an unusual situation for those of us in commercial life and those in government as well. It was just accepted by all of us as a way of life and was interesting in that we saw almost every corner of East Africa.

I was transferred to Kisumu in 1962 and this was because the company wanted our business to be developed and expanded in what Singers termed the *Lake District* which encompassed all the territory from Eldoret to Mwanza. A vast area where we had not concentrated on developing to our full potential. Very beautiful; stretching round a large proportion of Lake Victoria north and east. I had the pleasure of travelling to Eldoret, Kericho and Kisii – all at high altitude with chilly, fresh, cool air to breathe and then living in Kisumu on the shores of Lake Victoria, much lower down in altitude at 3,000 feet. I would normally drive to all my destinations which could be reached in less than a day. On a few occasions I did fly to Mwanza and this was when the road round the lake was closed due to heavy rains during the rainy season. On one occasion, I loaded my car on to the lake steamer *Victoria* at Mwanza (road from Mwanza closed due to heavy rain), and enjoyed a two-day voyage back to Kisumu stopping at Bukavu and Entebbe on the way. The *SS Victoria* was a lovely lake steamer which carried up to fifty passengers (as far as my memory serves me), with about twenty first class cabins and a large cargo hold and this vessel travelled round the entire lake once a week with its home port being Kisumu. The ship was built in England in pieces just large enough and no more, to fit into an East African Railways and Harbour's truck, then shipped from U.K. to Mombasa and then by train from there to Kisumu where all was pieced together, floated, and then fitted out. As the reader will appreciate – a marvellous feat of engineering which took place over a number of years.

Kisumu must have had a European population of not more than five hundred (my estimation) and consequently we all seemed to get to know one another. We had good friends, Ogwen and Penny Jones in Kericho which was only an hour's drive away. It was very pleasant for us to be able to travel there to enjoy the altitude and fresh air on the tea estate on which Ogwen was employed. They had three children of approximately the same age as ours, a large lovely residence, a club close by and fireplaces blazing with heat every night. This was all surrounded by masses of tea bushes.

In l962 our Kisumu had one chemist, one European doctor, one chief constable, one dentist, two motor dealers, one hotel (half a star probably), Singer shop and my main office, two banks, a saw mill and an air strip for planes up to the size of a Dakota to use. There were probably ten to twelve families of government employees living in government accommodation and the Provincial Commissioner who had a most imposing building housing his and his staff offices. One main street and oh yes, - a cinema, school, a couple of churches and a hospital. And that was about it, except for a few East African Railways and Harbours staff employed on the lake steamers. There were also a few Greeks and Indians who were sugar barons and all-in-all a fairly mixed cross-section of various types living very amicably in our Kisumu, shall we call it 'village'.

I was warned, soon after we arrived, to be careful when driving at night as there might be hippo roaming the streets. I suspected this might be a slight exaggeration to intimidate the newcomer as this warning came from the bar of the club where a lot of tall stories and pulling of legs took place. I was wrong. The hippo did roam the streets at night. I discovered that this was very frequent. It was fascinating to be driving along a tarmac road to see a hippo or two come out in front of one's car from the side of the road just taking a stroll in one's path. I took extreme care after finding out that the stories were indeed true, as a hippo is a big animal which could be injured and of course damage would result to one's car. As we all know, hippo will wallow in the water during the day. They come out at night to feed on any garden patches or edible grass as they are totally herbivorous.

There was an exceptionally unique phenomenon in Kisumu. The borough had adopted a herd of impala and these lovely creatures were protected and an absolute joy to the residents and would frequently visit our gardens and graze delicately until perhaps the resident dogs would chase them away. When they visited our garden we would keep our dogs indoors so that we could have the pleasure of watching them at close quarters, casually wandering through and sometimes pausing to graze on our lawn, not being in the least bit nervous! At times there were as many as twelve or fifteen and they found Kisumu easy to wander through from garden to garden as they just jumped over fences high and low with absolute ease. Early morning was the normal time that they visited and during the day they would inhabit the grassy fields surrounding Kisumu. I took a number of cine shots of them in our garden.

My home leave was due after only seven months of our arrival. We travelled to the UK and I have described that particular leave in detail in a previous chapter.

We returned after long leave, then took up residence in a different abode as the lease had expired on our 'close to club' house. Housing was difficult but we managed to find one which was large and luxurious – five bedrooms with a very big enclosed verandah and spacious garden with large lawns. Double storey with a view over the lake from upstairs where the large lounge and bedrooms were.

During my last two years in Nairobi the sport of go-karting had taken hold and I joined the club and bought a kart. A track had been built in Doonholme Road Stadium (no tarmac – murram only) and I became a big enthusiast and enjoyed the meetings where we enjoyed racing against each other - up to twenty at a time and perhaps forty or so in the club. Competition was keen as the kart engines were worked upon and became faster and faster.

There were other venues in Kenya where karts were racing - Nakuru, Sotik and most important of all, Kericho. As Kericho was only an hour from Kisumu, I decided to take my kart with me and perhaps approach the powers that be to race there. This decision turned out to be most auspicious as the arrival of my kart and the enthusiasm of the Kisumu crowd resulted in a number of new Kisumu drivers purchasing and racing in meetings at Kericho against the Kericho enthusiasts. Latterly we built a track at Kisumu which enabled us to hold meetings when Kericho visited and competed against us.

When we arrived at the new house I parked the kart on our large verandah and would frequently be making improvements to the engine and would start it up, making rather a racket as I tuned it.

We lived opposite the manager of Motor Mart and his family but did not meet for some weeks.

During a public holiday when all was quiet, a loud explosion occurred which sounded like a bomb detonating. It seemed to come from opposite; in other words, from our neighbours whom we had never met. I ran out on to the road and found that the explosion had not come from the house opposite but next door to the Motor Mart manager. I went into the garden as did a few other residents to find out what it was all about.

Allan Timms, whose wife was away at the time and who was catering for himself, was cooking his midday meal. He decided to heat a tin of peas inside the oven but without opening the tin. From memory I recall that the oven door had blown off and the wall opposite, left and right and also the ceiling, was splattered with green peas. The window was shattered.

We were all 'oohing and aahing' the results of this explosion when I was introduced to these new neighbours and others.

This was the beginning of a lifetime friendship with Dick (Richard McD Hodgson DSO) and Su Hodgson; he was the manager of Motor Mart.

As Dick was deeply entrenched in the motor industry and an engineer of excellence, having trained and studied in England, he was intrigued with the noise coming from opposite. He questioned me as to what the engine-revving was all about. One thing led to another very rapidly whereupon soon he was making all sorts of technical and highly-skilled improvements to my engine. Then he could no longer resist it and bought a go-kart himself. His expertise on engine 'souping up' resulted in our two karts being the fastest of all the karts in the areas of Kericho, Sotik and Kisumu.

Let us go back to Allan Timms. He was most fortunate not to be in the kitchen at the time of the explosion, so was not injured in any way.

The Hodgsons had three children of similar ages to our Graham and John and our families very rapidly became good friends. Dick, like me, was keen on hunting and fishing. Su was the daughter of Eric Sherbrook-Walker and The Lady Bettie Sherbrook-Walker. Eric, as all East Africans will know built Treetops at Nyeri.

Jack Dunkley, my bank manager, had introduced me to duck-shooting on the paddy fields on the lake shores and this latter sport took up a lot of my spare time, very happily.

Kisumu has a rather stable year-round climate although violent electric storms and heavy rain frequently occur at certain times of the year, especially in the evenings and we were able to gaze out at these spectacular turbulent storms from our view over the lake. The temperature of Kisumu is warm all the year round and this makes it a very agreeable place in which to live.

Shortly after our arrival in Kisumu, Dick and Su announced that a cousin of Su's would be arriving from London. One normally travelled from the UK to East Africa by either ship or by air. To our astonishment, Lady Clare Feilding (Su's cousin) was to arrive by road.

Clare had only just had her twenty first birthday and before that celebration was due to take place she was asked by her father – The Earl of Denbeigh, whether she would like a party or a trip abroad. She chose a journey to East Africa by overland and set off from UK travelling across the continent by train and then ship to Cairo where she embarked upon a Nile steamer starting a journey of epic proportions. The Aswan Dam had not been constructed at that time and so the vessel was able to proceed up-river and fairly far south. From memory I recall that she said that the Cairo steamer had taken her as far as Wadi Halfa and then partly by road and river steamer to Khartoum. After that there was a short distance up the White Nile to probably Malaka where she started a mammoth road journey in African buses, staying in roadside hotels (can you imagine?) which were primitive in the extreme.

On one occasion there was no hotel and she had to resort to relying on police hospitality by requesting a cell in which to sleep. No soft mattress but at least safe. Circumventing the Sud swamps she eventually arrived at Juba.

From Juba in the Sudan, she went all the way by African bus and night stops in African hotels once more; then to Nimule on the borders of the Sudan and Uganda and then into Uganda through Lira and Soroti staying at civilized hotels, but still travelling by African buses. The last lap was a short one from the Uganda border at Tororo to Kisumu where she disgorged from an African bus. Can you believe it?

This was to be the beginning of a lifetime in East Africa for Clare and she, like the rest of us, grew very quickly to love the country and its people, sliding into the lifestyle with ease.

As I mentioned earlier, we rapidly became friends with the Hodgsons and their children, Simon, Paul and Sonia. Su had relations farming at Ngobit and her parents lived close by at Naro Moru commuting to Tree Tops where Eric controlled everything. Su's aunt, The Lady Victoria Fletcher, and sister of Lady Bettie, farmed close by at Ngobit with her sons Christopher and Simon helping to run the large ranch-style farm concentrating on cattle.

Situated between Nanyuki and Nyeri, Naro Moru, nestling at the foot of Mount Kenya, is one of the most beautiful situations in Kenya at an altitude of six thousand feet which makes it a fabulous climate in which to live and particularly suitable for farming.

The Sherbrooke-Walker residence was designed by Eric and built by Italian prisoners-of-war soon after the second world war. It was a magnificent large residence built of grey granite stone, not double-storeyed but a long bungalow with all the rooms having a spectacular view of Mount Kenya. One unique aspect being an underground suite which Eric designed in case of any possible siege by the Mau Mau. The entrance was very cleverly concealed with a large granite-stone door and which could not possibly be detected as an entry to a very comfortable suite which could be stocked with food and lived in for some considerable time. The family never had to put it to use.

Soon after our arrival in Kisumu, Dick and Su invited us to travel in tandem to Lady Victoria's Ngobit ranch as she had invited the whole lot of us for Easter. Taffy, as Lady Victoria was affectionately known, had settled there years previously with her husband Miles and then separated. He went to farm elsewhere.

Let me describe 'Ol Taffeta' – Taffy's residence. Only a few miles from Eric Sherbrook-Walker's residence described above, Taffy's ranch enjoyed the flow of the Ngobit river which really is just a stream, fast flowing with an abundance of small trout. The big, rambling, *mabati* (corrugated iron) roofed house must have been built many years before, as it was an old-style Kenya farm residence with many rooms and a large verandah in front and to each side. Taffy kept a large surrounding garden with beautiful flowers in abundance and a big vegetable patch. There were spacious servants' quarters. Mount Kenya in all its glory was in full view. The extra large dining-room-cum-lounge was a place of many a convivial conversation, cleaning of guns and rifles, guests vying with dogs for a place to sit, sporting an electric button beneath Taffy's foot under the end of the dining table which summoned the serving waiters at her will during mealtimes through a bell in the kitchen.

Dogs were everywhere; she had seventeen of them and would frequently summon one of the servants to get rid of them to the verandah but of course, almost immediately this was done, they would sidle back surreptitiously and stretch out all over the carpets and trip up all and sundry until the trusty servant was re-summoned and the whole removal procedure gone through again.

Taffy was compassionate towards the Africans and particularly to her own servants and built a school not far from the house which was especially meant for the younger generation of early-age students of up to twelve years of age. All at her own expense - i.e. no government assistance. I cannot remember the acreage of the farm but it was huge, thousands upon thousands of acres. There were vast grazing lands for the Boran cattle which were the speciality which she bred. There was also a large proportion of land which was forest; inhabited by elephant, rhino, buffalo etc.

It was into this beautiful area of Kenya that we were introduced by Dick and Su. The first thing that Dick launched me into was fly-fishing, which was something I had never had the opportunity to enjoy before. He had advised me to take my little lake rod from Kisumu and this I did. I recall that the first stream that we fished was the Naro Moru near the Sherbrooke-Walker residence – a tiny stream only about four feet in width. It is to Dick that I owe a massive debt of gratitude as I have never stopped fly-fishing during these last forty-eight years and as I write I am enjoying the best fly-fishing in the world, here in England where I have retired and where this sport was first invented. His tuition was the best grounding I could ever have had.

Su's aunt, Taffy, presided over the events during our stay over Easter with a sense of humour and graciousness which is difficult to describe. She was one of the renowned 'characters' of East Africa who had started to farm with her husband, Miles Fletcher, some years before, and had cleared the land to make farming possible. They bought the land and did not 'steal' it as modern politicians and anti-colonialists will factually distort.

Miles Fletcher and Taffy parted in the early l95Os and she carried on through thick and thin with very little capital, purchasing 'Ol Taffeta' with the help of a government loan and a mortgage.

She and Miles met in l932 when she was asked to visit a hospital patient in Nairobi who had been hurt by an elephant.

Miles, an Australian from Tasmania was camped near Kajiado and had been commissioned by the Veterinary Department to make a survey of cattle in the Masai district with a view to inoculating them against the rampant killer disease of rinderpest.

One morning after breakfast, he left for his next place of inspection, on foot, leaving his camp boys to pack up and follow on after him.

After a mile from camp he was challenged by an elephant which had previously been wounded (as it was discovered later) and which charged. He was armed with an old-fashioned Paradox double barrel rifle which could fire shot or bullets. He had a camera in his shirt pocket. The elephant was so close and had caught him completely by surprise so that he had no time to bring the gun up to his shoulder. Consequently he raised it half-way up and then fired two bullets at its face. This just made it hesitate slightly and it carried on its charge, knocking him down and breaking his shoulder blade and some of his ribs. The irascible beast then turned and came back to finish him off; it first stabbed at him with its tusks whilst he was lying on the ground. The tusks fortunately impaled the ground on either side of him but wrecked the camera in his bush-shirt pocket. It then attempted to rub him into the ground with its trunk still held towards its chest and during this time Miles pretended to be dead. It stopped and then surveyed the situation and picked him up with its trunk and tossed him into a low thorn tree. Most chilling of all, he said to me, was that it then touched him all over whilst towering over him, with the tips of its prehensile trunk. This must have been only a short while but it seemed like an age to him. It then ceased investigating him with its trunk and trumpeted loudly and wandered off into the bush. He somehow managed to extricate himself from the scrubby thorn tree, collected his gun and started shuffling back to where his camp had been.

His camp crew then made a stretcher from his camp bed and started carrying him towards Namanga, which was closer than Kajiado. On the way he saw three elephants standing under a tree not far away and was relieved when his crew did not notice them as he reckoned they would have dropped him and run had they seen the elephants.

Eventually they arrived at Namanga and he was given primitive first-aid and part of this first-aid was to wash his thorn scratches with Lysol. The first-aid 'operators' had mistakenly thought that Lysol was a disinfectant. After this, an eight hour journey lying on the floor of a box-body car which must have been excruciatingly uncomfortable for him on such a rough road. Arriving at Kajiado he was attended to by the employees of a government outpost there. They summoned a small aircraft to fetch him but the pilot decided that the landing was too dangerous as there had been a recent downpour of rain and the airstrip was too wet.

Fortunately there was a railway station at Kajiado so he was taken to the siding by African government servants on his makeshift stretcher. One of the government employees had been instructed to stay with him to make sure he was loaded into the train when it arrived. This gallant gentleman, while waiting for the train to arrive, informed Miles that he was very thirsty and that he was therefore leaving him saying that many of the *bwanas* hurt by elephants had been brought to the station waiting for the train to arrive but most of them died before the train arrived, so he thought it a waste of time for him to stay with Miles and sauntered off to quench his thirst at the nearest beer hall!

Miles eventually arrived in Nairobi and was taken to hospital where yet another setback occurred when the only x-ray machine in the hospital being set up next to him was dropped. It was so badly damaged that no pictures could be taken of his broken bones. The nurses, during their spare time, used to come into his ward and pick out the thorns which were imbedded in his back and rear end.

It was at this stage that Taffy, who lived in Nairobi at that time, was asked to visit him. She would ride there on her horse to keep him company, and a romance started.

During the Mau Mau in the early fifties, the farmers in Kenya were targeted by this despicable organization. The motive – greed and envy. The targets – the softest. All farmers, situated at remote outposts with big distances between were at risk and those most vulnerable were those within the proximity of the forests, which acted as perfect bolt-holes for these terrorists.

Farmers barricaded their residences, put up watch towers, high fences with spikes on top, guards on watch, bright lights, electric fences and house alarms.

Not Taffy, who was at this stage divorced. She had none of those barricades and precautions installed. She did in fact sleep with her bedroom doors unlocked with those doors leading on to the verandah from her bedroom open. Yes, open, and none of those other precautions around the exterior of the house. However, she did have (approximately) seventeen guards inside her bedroom and some sleeping on her bed, a double one. Her guards were all canine. Although I asked her how many she had, she replied that she did not know but that the last time she counted the dogs was a few weeks ago and she thought there were about seventeen!! Upon further questioning she claimed that she slept very soundly, between fights!!

Another episode concerning Taffy was tax.

Before the Second World War, no income taxes were levied upon the residents of East Africa. It was a tax-free country but during the war when the Kenya government became bigger and more alert they suddenly discovered that nobody paid tax – (the British taxpayers were paying for the upkeep of the Kenya Colony government), the government gradually introduced all sorts of levies and stealth taxes until they decided to bring in income tax.

What a shock to all and sundry. Taffy was one of those who refused to pay. After prolonged postal altercations with no tax-collecting success in Taffy's case, the tax collectors moved in and visited her. She pointed out to them that legislation had not yet been passed in Legco (legislative council) approving the law to enable residents to be taxed and very politely asked them to leave. They had travelled a long way and intended to enforce their bosses' instructions to collect. Taffy then pulled out her double-barrelled twelve bore shotgun, loaded it and then threatened the worst if they did not remove themselves from her premises. She furthermore explained that if ever they visited again they would not be allowed through her gate!

When I questioned her about this story which had been doing the rounds, she dismissed it with a wave of her hand and a big smile. Such was our Taffy. What a lady!

8

Return to Nairobi

After two years in Kisumu we returned to Nairobi. I had completed the development and organization of Singers in the 'Lake District' in the area around Kisumu, as described earlier.

Promotion had been offered to me by returning to Nairobi. I was to be in charge of the whole of Kenya, Tanganyika and Zanzibar in our Head Office but under the direction of the General Manager of East Africa. Tanganyika and Zanzibar would be temporarily under my wing as the manager-in-charge of that area had left in a hurry and I would cover the gap until a replacement was found. Big scandal – he had vamoosed with one of the shop girls, not even white, and he being married. Tongues wagged incessantly, persistently, in perpetuity!

We had enjoyed our time in Kisumu which is a small town, even by East African standards. We made many friends, a number of whom became life-long friends like the Hodgsons, Dunkleys and Crossleys, to mention but a few.

It was therefore a wrench leaving Kisumu. To be back in the invigorating climate of Nairobi after the hot humid weather of Kisumu was a tonic. However, the most important aspect was the new challenge facing me. A vast area to cover.

Fortunately Cynthia is one of those marvellous souls who was able to adapt to all these big upheavals of household removals, new horizons, encountering new experiences, uprooting children from one environment to another, all with remarkable ease and forbearance.

Our head offices in Caltex House in Sadler Street were on the fifth floor and I had a luxurious office with large picture windows looking out over Nairobi. Alas, I was not to have much time looking out of windows. My new assignment required all my energies in dealing with the control of an ever-expanding business consisting of approximately sixteen shops in Kenya and a temporary extra half a dozen shops in Tanganyika and Zanzibar.

When I was not away flying to Dar es Salaam, Tanga, Zanzibar and other areas attending to the business there I was engrossed in Nairobi in sales figures, projects, expenses, profits, stock levels, staff strengths, visits from Singer dignitaries from New York and the United Kingdom, meetings, advertising and staff training schemes. The reader might think this was humdrum. It was not. On the contrary, when one becomes engrossed in the control, development and general running of a business entity large or small, it is to me the most absorbing pursuit in which one can have the privilege of being involved.

After approximately six months, a replacement was found to occupy the position of our philandering Tanganyika manager. This brought my workload back to some sort of normality. I was enjoying the cut and thrust of being in our Head Office in the 'big' city.

Mwingi hunt

I received a telephone call from my good friend Tony Marsh who was at that time stationed at Mwingi. He suggested that I should take a break from my hectic life in the great city and spend a short while hunting with him in the fresh country air of Mwingi. As Cynthia and I had never been as far north as that on the Garissa road and the two boys were at boarding school, I accepted the offer with alacrity even though the road, a good hundred miles of bone-shaking corrugations, had to be tackled. Tony was employed by the Agricultural Department of Kenya but was also an honorary game warden. Mwingi was therefore like a heaven-sent opportunity to him when the transfer was offered as the area was wild in the extreme and teeming with big game and elephant in particular. It was in Mwingi that his passion for elephant hunting started.

Let me describe Tony. He was a Welshman with a pronounced accent. Medium height with a slight weight problem which made him look a little 'soft' shall we say. Balding prematurely and sporting thick-lensed glasses. These characteristics concealed an athletic robustness which I was to discover to my dismay on some future elephant hunts with him. Tremendously alert in the bush, he observed and pointed out to me all manner of signs and observations which were interesting to hunters. As I was smoking at that period of my life and office-bound for long periods, I was not in the best physical shape and it was a desperate struggle to keep up with him when a fast pace was needed whilst tracking elephant.

I mean, Tony always set up a fast pace (his pace) and kept this up for hours on end and maybe sometimes all day.

Consequently my hip bones would be banging up into my armpits when he would show no signs of flagging and would carry on eagerly. However, self-esteem or ego is a marvellous invigorator and prods one on to heights of dexterity unimaginable under sane conditions. I always plodded on, determined not to show signs of wilting. Naturally I had expected an elephant hunt to be undertaken but I was wrong.

Rogue hippo

The District Commissioner of Mwingi had received a delegation of farmers protesting at the antics of a killer hippopotamus. This beast, they said, had plundered their maize fields for some time. The hippo is a herbivorous animal which normally wallows in water during daylight hours and grazes during the night.This looter however, had taken to marauding the maize at all hours, including daytime.

A farmer had perceived it walking into his maize field and munching his crop. This valiant yeoman had then approached the thief with a stone in one hand, a stout staff in the other and a loud voice.

Generally speaking, the hippopotamus is not an aggressive animal but there are exceptional circumstances under which it will attack human beings. The catalyst in this case was pure and simple – food. I could not blame the animal as it did not understand the laws pertaining to poaching. Even some human beings do not understand these laws.

The hippo, under a hail of abuse from stick, stone and voice, had decided that it would retaliate. It charged and must have taken a big bite at its assailant. Just one bite from that enormous mouth is sufficient to cut a man in half. He was found by his neighbours very badly wounded and did not recover.

The entire farming community was up in arms. This vicious culprit would have to be hunted down and destroyed. Why did not the Government annihilate the whole lot of these dangerous beasts? What use were they? Totally unfit to be farmers' neighbours. Could not the government understand this?

To placate the irascible local community of farmers, the District Commissioner had contacted Tony and instructed him to shoot a hippo. Any hippo. "For goodness sake, it does not matter which one did the dastardly deed, just eradicate one of them".

Tony acquainted me with the whole scenario upon my arrival. What did I think? Well I naturally expected us to be off on an elephant chase before the above facts were put to me. I therefore enquired "how many farmers are there and how many hippo?" The ratio was about 20 to 1 in favour of the farmers. "Yes," he said, his thinking was akin to mine but he pointed out that the deed had be done as the District Commissioner ordered.

I had never shot a hippo and had no desire to do so but I was keen to be with him in the bush for a while to get the big city cobwebs out of my mind. Cynthia remained behind and was entertained by Tony's charming wife.

We set off for the Tana River the following morning, together with all camping gear and three experienced boys (camp workers i.e. one *mpishi* and two helpers). This was government style camping and I realized how privileged government servants were when we arrived at the Tana river after about one hour's driving in Tony's Land Rover. He stepped out, gun-in-hand, beckoned me to follow and then shouted to his gentlemen *"tanganiza hema"* and off we went. Tanganiza hema meant – 'put up the tent'. It also meant a host of other things like putting the camp beds in place, making the beds, lighting a camp fire, heating water, preparing the next meal, chopping sufficient wood for the fire and making sure the cool box had sufficient beer for the evening. These three experienced old camping campaigners were taught by *Bwana* Tony. They did the job admirably and enjoyed it.

We approached the river and then parked a short way off and conferred with the chief's representative who was on the scene as we stopped the Land Rover. He had been waiting eagerly for our arrival. Tony was keen to get to the river in haste as we might have been embroiled with the mourners had we loitered and conferred.

The chief's reporter took us through the maize fields near the river and straight to the pool where the hippo were wallowing. "Oh yes," he said and pointed to a head which was amongst about seven or eight of them. "That's the one". I had grave doubts about his powers of observation and so did Tony as they all looked identical. It was not for us to argue but just to shoot. This would solve the problem.

It was a big pool above an island around which the water parted and flowed on either side down rapids with fairly large rocks protruding from the water.

Tony insisted I shoot as he said his eyesight was not good enough to locate the brain through the ear hole. They were about 35 to 40 yards away from us. I shot. There was a distinctive thud which we both heard. All the heads ducked under the water. Tony looked at his watch and noted the time carefully. He said that it would float in twenty minutes' time if I had found the brain shot. It was a soft-nosed bullet which I had used. The rest of the herd moved upriver under water and were not to be seen by us again.

In exactly twenty minutes something appeared near the rapids furthest away from us. Unfortunately there were a number of rocks in the water and we were unable to identify exactly whether what we saw was a rock or a hippo carcass.

The binoculars seemed to show that one of the rocks might be our quarry, lying on its side with tummy protruding slightly and water washing over it. We were unable to be sure.

It is not for me to narrate the foregoing hunt with any enthusiasm as I consider the hippopotamus to be a fascinating creature which should not be shot or eliminated but it had to be done and I was involved.

The reason that I have acquainted the reader with the hippo hunt is that it preceded a nerve-racking experience and acted as an introduction to what was to follow.

The Tana river was renowned for its large crocodile population.

Tony stared through the binoculars then put them down and thought for a moment - not long - and then suggested that the only way to find out whether our rock was really rock or hippo would be to swim over and investigate. "Swim," I asked? "You must be out of your mind" I mused that perhaps the sun had taken effect on his brain severely!

"Don't worry," he said, "I will swim over holding my rifle above my head whilst you cover me. When I arrive there you may follow me and I will cover you."

What sort of madness was this that he was suggesting? I looked all around for crocodiles but could see none. He saw me searching around. "Yes," he said, "They would not be here in this deep pool but below the rapids where it would be easier for them to spend less energy by just waiting for fish swimming upstream to pause before tackling the rapids and then devouring them."

I could not swim as fast as a fish and I thought that perhaps one of these reprehensible reptiles would be lurking in the big pool ready to devour my leg, torso or the whole of me. It was deep and the water was murky.

I looked around at the spectators – about six of them. All were waiting farmers who were anxious to see, first of all, whether their 'rogue' hippo would be despatched; but secondly to see the spectacle of one, or both of the *bwanas* being devoured! I suspected that the latter would be of more interest to them. I then approached them and suggested that as it was their rogue hippo which was to be located, that one, or all of them should swim over and find out. It was quite extraordinary. All claimed with poker faces that they could not swim!

Tony was eager to get going and was stripping down to his underpants. "Cover me. Shoot anything that moves" he said. He swam across, complete with rifle – and spectacles. Nothing moved.

It was now my turn and I stripped. Holding my rifle above my head I dog-paddled across. It was quite a long swim of perhaps forty or fifty yards but seemed like double that distance. He covered me.

Yes, it was our target and not a rock. Whether it was the rogue or not we will never know but that was highly unlikely. Tony signalled to the onlookers and I could see them rejoicing. The noise of the rapids drowned all sounds from them. They danced.

The hippo carcass is a valuable source of food to the African. There is an enormous amount of meat (quite unpalatable to the European) but perhaps of more importance is the huge amount of fat on the animal. When rendered down four *debbies* (sixteen gallons) of fat is collected. This is used as a cooking oil and is regarded as a great delicacy by the African tribes. The hippo also has a particularly hard pair of short tusks and this hippo ivory, as it is called, can be carved with a little more perseverance than elephant ivory which is much softer.

After the celebrating, these six gallant yeomen took swift action. They used two crude-looking hand-knives to pare the bark of a certain type of tree known to them. The bark came off in long narrow strips and they very adroitly plaited and twisted it into rope – bush style. I had never seen it done before. In about an hour the rope had grown to a distance which enabled Tony and I to tie the end round a front leg of the body so that these braves could then tug it towards them. Tony and I manoeuvred it round to the top end of the island and between rocks as they pulled. A long and laborious process before it was close enough for them to pull across the deep pool to the bank. Whilst this slow progress was going on I was able to get to close grips with, and inspect, an animal I had previously seen only at a distance. The skin is smooth and hard and of a reddish, purplish colour, blending into some dark brown areas.

We returned to Tony's residence the following day and he telephoned the District Commissioner advising him that his instructions had been carried out.

Two or three years after our episode, I was speaking to Mike Drury who had taken over the area as a permanent game ranger after Tony had been transferred. He confirmed that the sun must have affected Tony's brain severely to have contemplated such an episode.

One more Trotter

Cynthia was, at this time, expecting our third child. In those days, it was not possible to ask a doctor to use his ultra-sound detection equipment to determine the sex, as such marvellous contraptions did not exist. One used hocus-pocus contrivances. A gold chain with a ring on the end, held by hand, swinging over the stomach. If the chain swung in a circular movement in a clock-wise direction, the incumbent would be a girl, (if I remember correctly); and vice versa of course. Predictions were made, consultations held, learned opinion deliberated and wagers laid. Enquiries asking about the health of the *bwana* "standing the strain" were frequently asked. Naturally he would down an extra few pints every evening to help withstand the pressure of it all. Through all this, the *memsahib* would sail on serenely pampering all-and-sundry around her as though nothing unusual was taking place.

The great day was approaching and Cynthia had chosen the Princess Elizabeth Hospital for Women in Nairobi for her confinement. It was a lovely hospital in those days and probably the most up-to-date in East Africa.

Julia was born on the l0th July, l965. Big celebrations – after two sons.

In that era, there was no ban on flowers being presented and kept in the room of the young mother. There were another five or six young mothers in separate rooms, all having received many, many bouquets of the beautiful and colourful flowers found in abundance in Nairobi. Cynthia's room (ward), resembled a florist shop and extra small tables had to be brought in to accommodate the dozens of vases of blossoms. All went well. Mother and daughter - both glamorous – thrived.

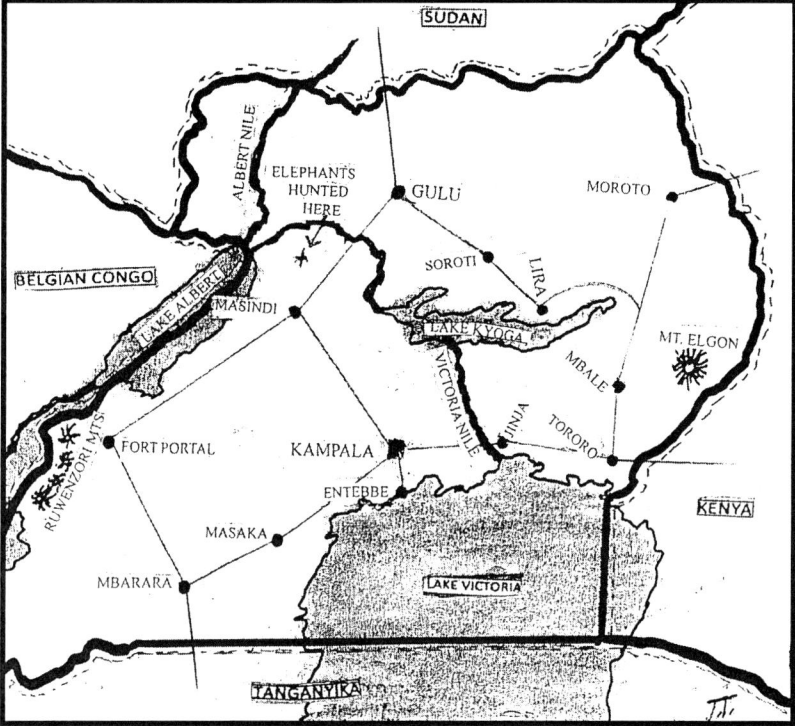

UGANDA

9

Kampala

Earthquake and an Army Coup

Nothing could be more contrasting than the comparison of Uganda with Kenya and Tanganyika. Uganda is a green, humid rainy country with the exception of the northern areas which are dry and open. The Mountains of the Moon to the west. Mount Elgon to the east.

In the last two years of my career in Singers, I held the power of attorney for the company and became General Manager in charge of all business in Uganda. We had thirty-three shops scattered over the country. I was to create a head office in Kampala to have a staff of forty including an accountant, sales supervisor, two secretaries, receptionist and clerks etc. Including shops, our Uganda organization would be a total of three hundred and forty employees.

I found on arrival on transfer that accommodation was at a premium and it took me two months of searching before I found a suitable residence.

During that time, my number two – George De Balman – took me to all the shops. I immediately took a liking to him and this augured well for our working together. He was hard-working, born and brought up in Uganda, keen on his job and knew the country better than anyone. Young and newly married he was the ideal man to have close under me.

I set to work creating our new Uganda head office. My accountant, Alan Lawson soon arrived to settle in and set up our accounting section, interviewing and appointing thirty clerical applicants.

He was yet another staff asset: young (twenty eight years old), qualified, unassuming and full of humour. Particularly sharp. Being unmarried and not knowing anyone he soon became a personal friend of our family. Alan was born and educated in England where he qualified as a chartered accountant, hated the weather, decided to take the plunge and applied for a job which we had advertised in East Africa. I was fortunate that our head office in Nairobi had assigned him to me.

Within a period of about six months to a year, the whole operation was turned into an effective autonomous division of Singers in East Africa.

As head of our operations in Uganda, I would quite frequently receive letters addressed to me on a variety of subjects concerning our business. One gem I must relate concerned a seriously worried father. I quote from memory.

> "Honoured Sir, it is with grate impassion that this letter is passed to you. It is to complaned your shop manager in Masaka. Last week he did drive near my dauter and give her lift on journey. Unfortunatley, he did drive into the bush and then stop and enlope her in back of Singer van. Now this is big problem because she was virgin but no longer. Dowry was to be for cows but not now, only one. That means for cows is Shilling 400.00 for me to get not.This is now my intention that Singer must pay me Shilling 400.00 for what I lost in back of your van
>
> Please pass me the money quick as it is my wish to buy another wife with that money.
>
> Yours very truly,"

Naturally all letters had to be answered and I did enjoy writing a reply. The word *enlope* was particularly fascinating to me. My secretary found it difficult to take down the reply when I dictated. She was in stitches of laughter.

My arrival in Uganda coincided with a political upheaval of no small significance. The Kabaka was being overthrown. All was in a state of turmoil. I had gone ahead of my family and stayed in a small flat whilst looking for a residence in which to live.

It was always a pleasure to go on business safaris and I felt that to be personally contacting the shops and their problems or successes, or both, was most rewarding. It gave me a closer and better grasp of the business at grass roots level. I could traverse the northern areas in one week and the southern areas in ten days. Travelling by car over these vast areas as far as Gulu and Moroto in the north; in the south as far as Mbarara; was made most comfortable in the evenings by staying at the Uganda hotels. This chain of hotels was renowned throughout East Africa for its cuisine, good clean comfort and excellent service.

Travelling with George de Balman on one occasion we arrived at Masindi Port and checked into the hotel, lunched and then spent the afternoon visiting the shop and checking the relevant records. The manager was an excellent man and had only a few problems so that we could complete our visit and prepare for an early start next morning for Fort Portal.

At six o'clock the following morning I was awakened by a violent shaking. It did not take me long to realize that an earthquake was taking place. I rushed outside, pyjama clad only. George had beaten me to it from his room which was next to mine and was standing there looking at the building. We both foolishly stood there watching the shaking. I say foolishly because had the earthquake become more intense and the building collapsed, we would have been engulfed under the rubble. The hotel was a few storeys high and we were situated on the ground floor. As the aftershocks came every five minutes, we decided to skip breakfast and seek safer territory in Fort Portal.

Arriving at Fort Portal we discovered that the town was in turmoil. It had been fairly badly hit (5.2 on the Richter scale) and the first thing we did was to see if our shop was damaged. From the outside it looked perfectly normal to me. I asked the manager how things were and he pointed out a crack along one side of the mezzanine floor saying that the shaking had been rather violent. As our building was good and strong it had not been as badly hit as the palace of the King of Bunyoro (I think Bunyoro). Apparently it had suffered serious damage and large parts had eventually to be rebuilt. The chimney on the building which housed the Standard Bank had tumbled down and fallen on to the road not far from our shop. Apparently no serious injuries had occurred in the town.

The office in our shop was situated on a mezzanine floor at the rear with steps leading up to it. After reviewing the frightening early-morning earthquake events with the manager and his staff and making an inspection all round I decided to check the office records. George and I then went up the steps to settle in to the business of cashbook, stock records etc.

At approximately two p.m. we were engrossed in our work when a loud roaring noise akin to that of an express train approaching at high speed, met our ears. I was at a loss but the manager was not. He shouted to George and me to get outside and was first to scamper down the stairs and outside through the front doors. The two clerks, manager, George and myself together with sales staff, stood outside looking at the shaking. The manager knew exactly what it was when the roaring started as the same had been heard when the first quake struck during the morning prior to our arrival.

At intervals of five minutes, aftershock tremors then took place. I thought it would be more conducive to ensure our longevity by taking the hire purchase ledgers to the hotel and work on their verandah under a *mabati* (corrugated iron) roof instead of having bricks and mortar around us. We advised the manager to close the shop and allow the staff to go home. The regularity of the aftershock tremors was unnerving but we managed to complete our work. The manager and clerk who were working with us returned the ledgers to the shop.

I decided on a bath before dinner but this posed a problem. The bathroom was, of course, in the building adjoining my room, all concrete. How strong? George announced he would go straight to the bar, it was safer. One could bolt out across the verandah, drink in hand, before the express train struck the pub.

My dilemma was either to follow his example or to perform what I had done for many years – a bath before drinks and dinner. I decided on the latter as I hate change.

I had a plan in view. Rather than attempt a high-speed sprint from bathroom to verandah sans attire, I would, when the train arrived and the roof caved in, hug the bottom of the bath and the high sides would protect me. Help would then be able to be summoned by letting the water out and shouting through the plughole.

Nothing happened. Only the continued pattern of the aftershock tremors.

A very hurried bath enabled me to proceed to the bar post-haste and join George. He said he was doing his best to become as immune as possible to the thought of being run over by a train, in bed. Alcohol would be the answer he opined and downed another drink. I cannot remember exactly how many we had but it must have been effective. At breakfast the following morning we agreed that the medicine of the night before had worked admirably although it was somewhat harsh.

An Ugly Incident.

As mentioned earlier, in l967, the Ugandan government was in the throes of a coup.

When Uganda became independent, the British government had decided (in its wisdom) to split the premiership of the country in two. Instead of a single Prime Minister or President, a shared control of the country between the King and the Prime Minister was created. (Shakespeare would have commented "strange bedfellows").

King Freddie of Buganda and politician Milton Obote were the grandiloquent appointees in this partnership. Can you imagine it? The Kabaka and Obote dancing in concert to the same drum beat!!

A period of spurious bonhomie then wobbled along for some time before antagonism reared its ugly head. Obote, during this time, had been colluding with the 'defence minister' Onama, with a view to removing Freddie. Obote was of the Langa tribe from Gulu in the north and he made sure that the army was almost entirely recruited from that area. Naturally the King was a Bugandan – a tribe used to ruling the largest tribal kingdom in Uganda, with his palace in Kampala which as we all know is in the south-east of the country.

The King only rarely left Uganda to visit England where he was educated at public school and Oxford. Whether Obote wanted to depose him in a coup or eliminate him we will never know.

The upshot of all this was that the great Ugandan army rose against King Freddie and his palace troops. The latter consisted of a handful of ceremonial foot-soldiers poorly equipped with out-dated rifles (old 3O3s). These soldiers were dedicated to their King and the Kingdom of Buganda. They defended stoutly. Obote seized the radio and television station and announced that he was now in sole command. Thus a classical African tribal conflict situation had commenced.

This was mid l967 when I arrived from Nairobi to take up my new position in Singers. I kept Cynthia and the children in Nairobi as I hoped the situation would resolve one way or another to enable sanity and stability to return.

Ignoring the situation around me I plunged into my new job. The whole of Kampala rapidly grew more and more tense as shooting started to be heard. All our African staff were becoming increasingly uneasy. They constantly passed on rumours and facts of fighting beginning all around us. Kampala took on a hushed mantle of fear but no fighting was visible on the streets of the city itself. Information reached us that road blocks had been set up on all arterial roads leading into and out of Kampala. We were virtually isolated from the outside world.

As this situation was at this point affecting our business I decided to investigate the validity of these stories by having a closer look. I took my Sales Manager, George de Balman and two District Managers, Drake Baale and Otis Seremunye to one of the road blocks that everyone was talking about. Baale and Seremunye were Bugandans. We travelled towards Kalolo Hill where the noise of gunfire seemed to be prevalent. The Palace of the *Kabaka* (King) was perched on the top of this hill.

Small houses littered this area and we did a substantial amount of business in all the surrounding villages at the base of Kalolo Hill. I drove my Peugeot with my three passengers on the main road leading to the Palace. All seemed tranquil. I expected to see a road block when nearing the base of the hill – but nothing akin to a roadblock appeared. All seemed quiet, but too quiet.

We travelled another half mile perhaps, when Baale screamed at me "stop, stop". I stopped. A Ugandan soldier had leapt out of a bush close to the road on the left side of the car. He ran the few yards from the bush towards the front left passenger window where George sat, pointing his Kalashnikov into the open window, yelling hysterically at us to get out.

This command mobilized us rapidly and we all disembarked. Baale and Seremunye then stood stock-still, with their arms pointing outwards. Have you ever seen the black of an African's skin turn grey? Their complexion took on a distinctive hue of pale grey as they stood petrified. At this stage the soldier directed his weapon from left to right at the approximate height of our stomachs. He was about seven or eight feet in front of us. As I looked at him I noticed that he was very young – perhaps seventeen or eighteen. His hands were shaking uncontrollably. Around his waist was a wide webbing belt and underneath this he had pushed up the solid end of a thick steel cable. The other end of the cable was frayed. I would think that the cable was a little thicker than my thumb at the end which was not frayed.

George stood there with a terrified look on his face and froze into a state of total moribundity.

We faced this frenzied soldier like sitting ducks and I realized that the only weapon available to us was my tongue.

This young soldier of the Ugandan Army then shouted at us in English in a high-pitched voice accusing us of being "spies". He ranted on until I explained that I was the head of the Singer organization in Uganda and that we had proceeded into this area to assess the effect that the fighting would have on our business.

He then turned on Baale and Seremunye asking them in English whether they were Bugandans. Baale made the error of replying that he was a Langa from Gulu. This reply was given in the mistaken belief that the soldier would be sympathetic towards him. The young soldier then rattled off a few questions in the Langa language and immediately perceived that Baale was unable to reply. Our crazed young soldier acted quickly and correctly accused Baale of being a Bugandan. Pulling the frayed steel cable from his belt he struck our Baale across the chest with the frayed end, twice. I remonstrated with him and he then swung his Kalashnikov pointing it at my stomach with finger on the trigger, again accusing us of being spies.

At this stage I could see through his nylon shirt pocket that Baale had a Singer business card. I told him to take the card out and show it to the soldier. He could not move and stood there paralysed. I stepped towards him and plucked it out and handed the business card to the soldier. At this stage, the Kalashnikov muzzle was less than a foot from my stomach. It occurred to me at that point that I could easily grab the barrel and deflect its direction so that the other three, and myself could overpower this unhinged youngster. I resisted this temptation.

At this juncture when I continued talking, talking and talking in order to try and allay his suspicions or calm him down in some way; he shouted to me to be quiet. He did, as he told me to be quiet, look past me at the crest of a small hill close behind me. Through the silence we could hear a crowd approaching.

The crowd advancing then, thankfully occupied his attention and he screamed at us to remove ourselves. We were not slow in jumping into the car. I reversed off the road and proceeded to turn around when I noticed that I had almost run over a body lying on the ground. The pieces then fell into place in my mind as to why he was so jumpy and nervous. He must have done his first killing shortly before our arrival.

But what appalled me was that the body could not have been more than fourteen years old, poorly clad — very worn tackies, grubby khaki shorts and a threadbare blue shirt.

This was not the end of this very ugly confrontation. As we started to draw away from the place of the incident, Seremunye pointed out another soldier concealed, armed and crouching behind a bush not far from where we had passed on our way up the hill. This soldier had been back-up for his comrade in case the latter had been unable to handle the situation with us. Any action which I had contemplated would have been covered by this reserve auxiliary.

This frightful contretemps had demonstrated to me the deranged depths into which primitive man will plunge when the power of the barrel of a gun is placed in his hands.

The Kabaka is Overthrown.

Kampala did actually become isolated although we were able to move through road blocks if on business.

A curfew was imposed on all residents from six p.m. until six a.m. I was safely ensconced in the Imperial Hotel on the first floor and this gave me a good view of proceedings in the centre of the city and also a panoramic view of Kalolo Hill. The Kabaka's Palace was perched on the top of this hill.

The days following our incident described above developed into more and more frequent gunfire being heard. Most of it seemed to be around the area of Kalolo Hill and I took some cine shots from the balcony outside my room in the hotel.

Army trucks were to be seen everywhere; guns bristling.

Where was the Kabaka? Rumours flew. He was personally directing army operations from his Palace defences. He was facing Obote's rabble Langa troops in person at the head of his own valiant defenders! These Langa savages were being repulsed time and again! Heroic deeds by the Palace troop guards took place daily, hourly! Long live the Kabaka! What a grand fellow!

More disturbing than the rumours was the sight of army traffic traversing the roads at high speed. All drove at a velocity way in excess of the speed limit. Traffic lights were totally ignored. It was not a pleasant place to be – driving on the roads. I rose earlier than usual and hastened to the office before 6.30 each morning. A large number of trucks contained troops in the rear – all heading in the direction of Kalolo Hill. But what did those returning carry? Nothing could be seen except that some seemed to be heavily laden. The natural conclusion of the onlookers was that they contained bodies. Further rumours – blood could be seen dripping from the rear of some. Word reached us that bulldozers were digging great holes outside the city. Telephone communication was cut off.

I found that the two shops and *godown* in Kampala were now filled with staff all in a state of panic and dread. Naturally they were all terrified of what was taking place and huddled in small groups whispering. Those who lived outside the precincts of the town had found friends in Kampala with whom they could sleep at night as it was much too risky to travel outside the boundary. In any case, road blocks stopped traffic and buses were not operating.

My worst fear was that shop looting might begin. As I mentioned earlier the army was mostly made up of troops recruited from the Northern areas of Gulu and they were raw and uncivilized.

We closed the two shops and *godown*. The only thing I could think of to do was to keep their minds off the present situation as much as possible. I went with George to the shops and we started everyone – the shop managers included, practising their skills at machine demonstrating. The machine embroidery departments were set to teach those members of the staff, salesmen included, who had no skills in this art.

A large window in my office looked out and down from the first floor to a rather busy traffic intersection. By chance I had brought my cine camera with me. When once I gazed out of the window wondering where and when this was all going to end, I heard and then observed a Land Rover blowing its horn frantically at an ordinary saloon car which had blocked its path. The car had stopped on the red of the traffic light and this had prevented the Land Rover from proceeding.

The hooting stopped. A very smart and important-looking officer disembarked from the Land Rover and swaggered forward with a nonchalant and most impressionable gait, Kalashnikov in hand. Our gallant Uganda army was now able to be observed in its full splendour going into action. I grabbed the cine camera. He arrived at the driver's window of the car ahead. A very nervous-looking young white lady was the occupant and she listened to his words, I could see, in fear and trembling.

Her guilt was that she had had the temerity to block the path of a vehicle carrying an officer of the Ugandan army. He was giving her a severe lecture on the seriousness of her transgression. One can imagine the gist of the conversation. "Whata you think you doing?" "I just stopped at the red light Sir". "Andaa yous think that this liddle light is a more important thana the officer of the Ugandan army?" And so on, but let us not denigrate this splendid intrepid icon of Uganda's defence of the realm.

I carried on filming until he re-entered his Land Rover. His driver then drove him away.

The Uganda army and naturally the Kabaka's troops had no heavy equipment such as tanks or armoured cars. Obote's troops did have jeeps with heavy machine guns. They also possessed bazookas and it was spectacular seeing the explosions from these rockets exploding on the Palace. One out of every three found its mark! It started burning with a plume of smoke rising high into the sky. I have a good cine shot of this.

Shortly after Obote announced on the radio that he had taken command - he appeared on television. This was a few days after I had filmed the smoke rising from the burning Palace.

The interviewer was, I think, from a UK newspaper. He asked where the Kabaka was and Obote replied that his troops had not yet captured him. "But your troops claim to have captured the Palace. Where is he and what will you do when and if you do capture him?", he asked. Obote replied, "Our brave soldiers have defeated the Palace troops. When we catch him we will question him". "And then?" asked the interviewer. "We will let him go", said Obote.

King Freddie who obviously did not have much faith in the sincerity of his erstwhile governing partner, climbed through a bathroom window in the dead of night and scarpered post-haste. We never heard exactly how he travelled but a few weeks later he turned up in the UK.

A further TV interview took place after the one described above. Obote pronounced himself to be President of the great new Uganda. A new era was to begin! Questions were asked by reporters. "Why did it take you so long to capture the Palace Mr. President?" "Wella our troops were delayed by the rain". "The rain Mr. President did I hear you say?" "Yes, naturally our troops could not proceed with this rain coming out of the sky so we waited until it stopped". The reporter then delivered his coup de grâce and asked – "Mr. President, does the Uganda Army have raincoats?" The import of the question was lost upon our honourable, self-proclaimed new leader of Uganda and the interview continued.

"Where is the Kabaka?" asked another of these hardened questioners; they were enjoying this. "Well, we have not found him yet but mark my words we will catch him". The reporter - "We understand that he has eluded your ring of troops around the Palace and left the country". "Don't you believe those-a-rumours, because we will get him, yes we will get him."

Thus, our new President entered into the leadership of Uganda. Although sporadic gunfire continued for some days, things returned to some sort of normality within a week or so.

With Obote from the north in charge, an uneasy calm prevailed. He ruled with an iron fist; or through the barrel of the gun. Any dissension or slight resistance was rapidly quelled by army thugs who eliminated any suspect, be he politician, soldier or public servant. No opposition party existed.

An assassination attempt was made on the President; all was hushed up. He was travelling on the road between Port Bell and Kampala. This road passes close to Mbuyu Hill where we lived and where a large army barracks was perched on the summit. Our house was at the foot of the hill and about one hundred yards from the Port Bell/Kampala roads.

A machine gun was set up on the road at a point not far from us by whom we know not. Its sights and barrel covered any vehicle coming from Port Bell. It was set up during the night when word was whispered to the would-be assassins that a motorcade carrying the President from Port Bell would be proceeding. Motor cycles preceded the cavalcade. The President, it was calculated by those scheming to be rid of his Excellency, would be in either the first or second car. Usually this great dignitary travelled in a cavalcade of five or six cars – three black Mercedes in front; the third, not so good looking as it must have been picked up at some second-hand dealer's yard. It looked decidedly tatty when parading the streets of Kampala. The last two or three cars were old *gharries* of motley appearance, not Mercedes.

The lookout alerted the 'marksman' that the cavalcade was approaching. He opened fire on the first two and let go a hail of bullets killing, we don't know whom. Obote had outwitted the plotters by riding in one of the old velocipedes at the rear. His 'intelligence' department must have alerted him, perhaps.

Hush, everyone knew about it but none dared utter it out aloud. The local paper, (Kampala Herald, I think), was not allowed to print any information whatsoever concerning this assassination attempt.

Life did eventually continue normally after some months but of course the Bugandans would not accept a ruler from the north after having been ruled by their Kabakas for more than a century. A very disgruntled Buganda therefore was forced to accept the situation under Milton Obote; in fact they had no option as his brutal regime brooked no dissent.

I did my best to ignore all these political shenanigans and put all my energies into the new venture challenging me.

As things calmed I brought Cynthia and the family from Nairobi. At this stage we were a family with three children. Michael had not yet been born. It was a year later that he was born in Mulago Hospital. My mother-in-law came to Kampala and very kindly looked after us during Cynthia's confinement.

Graham and John had been entered into Kenton College in Nairobi at the beginning of the year prior to our departure to Uganda. It was therefore necessary to fly them to and fro for holidays and the end-of-year break.

Julia was a two-year-old and being looked after by Sinabu, an excellent *aya* who had worked for Mickey and Margaret Shaw bringing up their children. We encouraged her to speak as much Swahili to Julia as possible so that she would learn the language. What happened was that she learned Kiswahili much quicker than English and spoke more Swahili than English in her very early years.

Life continued as normally as possible under the existing conditions but an uneasy calm reigned.

I had witnessed, at close quarters, the ease with which a calm situation could explode in a country like Uganda. I had also partially seen the upheaval of the Mau Mau in Kenya.

It was in this atmosphere of political and military volatility that Cynthia and I agonized about a move to calmer climes.

We sadly decided to leave East Africa. However, we had spent a great deal of our lives in these three lovely countries and look back on those years as some of the best of our lives.

10

The Budongo Forest

For close on twenty years in East Africa I had hunted at every opportunity and bagged a fairly good cross-section of antelope and big game, some of it dangerous which was exceedingly thrilling to hunt and eventually bring down.

As mentioned previously, Uganda had suffered the effects of the upheaval of the overthrow of the Kabaka. Milton Obote had seized power. All was in a state of tension and chaos, with the army everywhere flexing its muscles in a most remarkable way. Every soldier was a self-appointed authority and sporting one of an array of imposing weapons – AK47s, rifles, revolvers, tommy-guns; - and adopted a swagger of self-importance which was most impressive. New proclamations were pronounced daily by a number of dignitaries in Government most of which conflicted with each other. The redoubtable Idi Amin was appointed chief of the 'armed forces'!

It was in this atmosphere that we lived and it was in this atmosphere that I became embroiled in applying for a licence to shoot an elephant in Uganda. As I have previously written I had to apply to, and obtain the permission of, none other than the Minister of Defence to bring a .375 rifle and l2 gauge shotgun into Uganda two years previously. That had been a series of tough and sometimes humorous negotiations; haggling, consulting, persuading and eventually obtaining a written letter from that great dignitary. I did not resort to any bribery as this had not yet become fashionable.

Honourable good old-fashioned customs inherited from British colonial rule still reigned in the late 1960s.

The dignitary to whom I was to make my application was one Felix Onama, Minister of Defence. I had previously met him in a bar whilst rubbing shoulders with him over a beer or two. He had patronizingly advised me to never again engage in the perilous habit I had of hunting in Karamoja as either of those two redoubtable antagonists, the Dodoth or the Dodong, who were at war with each other, would surprise me at night and spear me to death!

In any event, I did not have to meet him but if I had done so I would have reminded him of what great buddies we were, having a beer together in that dubious bar and how he had saved my life by giving me such excellent advice on the ferocity of the antagonists in the great Karamoja war.

I was, of course, fobbed off from one office to another and being told "come back next week" a number of times, until I eventually arrived in the office of the secretary of the great man himself. She accepted my application, which was in the form of an ordinary letter and promised to present it to the minister and would advise me, in writing, of his decision. I waited and waited and then after five or six weeks, returned to her when she graciously and with an air of great importance, handed this epistle over to me saying that all had been approved. The date of the letter indicated that it had been lying on her desk for a number of weeks!!

The area in which I had requested to hunt was under the jurisdiction of the District Commissioner at Masindi. This gave me a vast area in which to hopefully find a good pair of tusks.

My next-door-neighbour, George Palmer, a dentist and avid hunter like myself, was keen to accompany me but had unfortunately recently had an operation on one of his lungs and could not undertake any arduous walking safaris such as elephant hunting. However, he did have a pal with whom he had done some hunting, but short episodes, all after small game. This friend was keen to accompany me. He was an Indian gentleman who possessed a rifle of approximately the same calibre as my own.

I was happy to let him accompany me as it might be safer to have some back-up. I decided first of all to go into the Budongo Forest as I had heard that bush elephant were plentiful but that heavy tusks might be hard to find. This was in early March 1969. The Budongo forest was an untouched and preserved national forest which had never been inhabited, measuring one hundred miles in length by fifty miles in width. The trees absolutely magnificent, mostly muvule (Chlorophhora Excelsa, so my East African learned friend Ken Sargent told me on a holiday to Cornwall at the time of writing in 2006), stretching up hundreds of feet and all with very large impressive buttresses for at least 30 to 40 feet from the ground upwards. The foliage at the top was dense so that only a minimum amount of light penetrated into this murky world.

We arrived on the edge of this protected sylvan phenomenon in my sturdy Peugeot station-wagon mid-afternoon and set up camp, to be ready, hopefully to find a tracker and set off on the morrow. There was a little human habitation on the edge of the forest with some simple *shamba* activity not far from where we camped. The sight of the forest was formidable. Looking at the edge of this unusual hunting-ground I decided that some local knowledge of the terrain, which was rather hilly, would be necessary to track and then engage the elephant. We were told that other big game, such as buffalo also inhabited the area. The following day was spent hunting for a tracker – we found one (name unpronounceable) and were surprised to have a government employed game scout tag on to our party. Both informed me that they were conversant with the geography inside the forest and the tracker claimed to have lived on his *shamba* close by for many years. This lucky find seemed to augment our chances of good hunting for the next few days.

The following day we set off early at sunrise and the tracker kept up a lively pace. I was in awe of the massive trees but we did not see any signs of the elephant habitation for some hours and during these first few hours, the going was becoming tougher and tougher with many gullies to cross. It meant sliding down one side, climbing the other, continually. Eventually signs of elephant activity were becoming apparent; such as lesser trees having been felled recently by the jumbos. Lying across our path were heavier logs that we were continually bending under or clambering over. Our tracker was now slowing down and testing the wind and listening carefully. About noon it became obvious that we were nearing a herd and could clearly hear them – tummies rumbling, trees crashing and branches being pulled and pushed. Pulses quickened with tension and excitement mounted as we crept closer and closer to these sounds. The scrub bush under the big trees was fairly thick and although we seemed to be almost into the herd, it was not possible to identify the sizes of tusks as we were unable to go much

Ken with Muvule Bowl

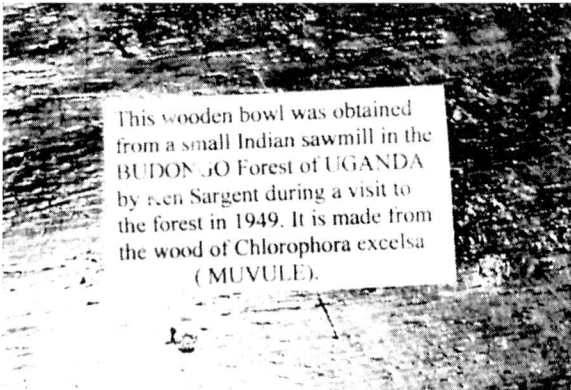

This wooden bowl was obtained
from a small Indian sawmill in the
BUDONGO Forest of UGANDA
by Ken Sargent during a visit to
the forest in 1949. It is made from
the wood of Chlorophora excelsa
(MUVULE).

Inscription on bowl

further and even if we had gone only a few yards further we would have been bumping into them. All this was most frustrating, being so close and unable to see a thing. I thought of climbing, or inducing our tracker to climb a tree for a possible sight of any worthwhile tusks but he declined, thinking it too risky. What could we do? Only one thing and that was to creep and I mean creep, closer and closer. Throughout this five or ten minutes of indecision and frustration the elephants continued to crash around; rumbling tummies and sometimes low-pitched trumpeting filled the air right in front of us. Then something extraordinary happened which was unexpected; the tracker stopped dead in his tracks and pointed gently to his left and slightly ahead. At first I could see nothing in the murky shadows and bush where he was pointing. Then I saw it – the rear end of an elephant cow dozing or sleeping. But we were just about on top of her – only four or five feet away. I could not believe what my eyes were shouting at me as it was so close. In a flash I realized what marvellous camouflage these enormous beasts enjoy in their own environment but I also thought that this was far too close for comfort and the tracker and I very carefully engaged reverse gear, putting ourselves at a distance which would enable me to take aim and fire if she turned and charged. The Indian hunter and game scout also retreated behind the tracker and myself. I might mention at this stage that I was the only one who had a licence to kill an elephant.

In order to obtain a view of the size of her tusks I moved sideways. Even if the tusks were a good size I could not have shot her as one did not shoot cows, only bull elephants. However, I was curious to see what the bush elephants carried in the way of tusks and hence my moving to the side to obtain a view of the ivory. Well. She just had little pegs and as I looked at her head sideways on, she must have either seen or smelled me (or us) and she swung around, to my dismay. I would have been obliged to shoot if she charged. It was later after the event that my tracker confirmed that there was a light puff of wind which had blown towards her and it would have been this that alerted her, carrying our scent.

It was now me or her and I stood there with rifle ready to fire if she made a move towards us. It is quite extraordinary and difficult to comprehend how elephants communicate with each other. She did not make a sound but the rest of the herd got the message that we were there and immediately stopped all feeding activity so that the crashing around noisily, tummy-rumbling and vocal noises all ceased promptly and were replaced by the very gentle noises of the rough elephant skin scraping against bushes as the herd moved away from us quickly. Did she alert the herd unbeknown to us, and without a sound to them by some means known only to the elephants? Perhaps Dame Daphne Sheldrick could throw some light on this.

Another action which I think worth mentioning is the speed at which she swung round and confronted me. It is in the winking of an eye that these great heavy beasts can turn and defend their position without making a sound.

She just stood poised, trunk held back towards her chest and staring at me while the rest of our party quietly retreated. I expected a charge but fortunately it did not come and she slowly and elegantly turned and walked away with tail swaying from side to side and then breaking into a run to catch up with the herd. There was now an eerie silence and all tension relaxed in this peaceful, quiet, beautiful forest. Pulses returned to normal. This was a very big experience for me. Heavy evidence of sweating palms – mine.

We sat down and reviewed the situation. I also walked around and looked at the area in which they had been feeding so blissfully. Trees up to six inches thick had been knocked over and the leaves partly devoured; bark had been stripped from smaller and larger trees and a considerable amount of dung deposited all around, some of it still steaming.

The lessons learned amounted to one very clear answer to my search for an elephant with a good pair of tusks. No more thick bush hunting in the murky light of the Budongo Forest! Bush elephant tusks are generally smaller than those of the open plains; the poor visibility made it almost impossible to select a pair of tusks, if they existed in a herd. There was the added difficulty of obtaining a clear shot. If I were an elephant I would never have moved from the Budongo Forest!

We had spent the best part of six hours tracking that herd so a long trek now lay ahead of us back to camp. Relying on the credentials of our tracker, we set off.

The ground in the Budongo Forest is always damp, and slipping and sliding was just part of the general difficulty of making our way. I recall that my khaki shirt was torn in all sorts of places by the thorns, my one trouser leg had a tear in it in the front, from thigh height right down so that it flapped behind me as I walked. I wore a hat but it was continually dislodged by thorns so that I frequently took it off to put in my pocket which meant that the top of my head became impaled and scratched by thorns. Some thorns cutting and others, not many, lodging in my scalp. Face, arms, chest and one leg all scratched, muddy and with the odd spot of blood visible here and there. I looked at myself and laughed and laughed as it reminded me of one of those films where the 'hero' would be portrayed emerging from some desperate venture, probably in a forest, looking as haggard as myself.

The return journey started and then we slipped and slithered, crawled, jumped over and crouched on our way for a number of hours. After the excitement of the chase this part of the hunt always seems to be more arduous as there is no longer a quarry to be tracked or a goal to be reached. It was now mid- afternoon. I could see that my crew were beginning to bend under the weight of the day's march. They did not have the adrenalin pumping through them as I did so this made the venture more tiring for them.

At that stage in my life I could boast of being incredibly fit and could out-walk a tracker with ease so, although I looked like a mess, as we all did, I was not really exhausted as they seemed to be.

I called a halt and we sat down, not having had anything to eat since breakfast. After a break of twenty minutes we carried on and the return journey seemed never-ending when suddenly I noticed a broken tree lying down which we had seen before. I looked a wee bit closer and mentioned this to our party. The tracker now looked embarrassed. After we discovered footmarks (of our own) and I thought about a few other signs; it was obvious that his sense of direction had eluded him. But he insisted that he knew where we were so we followed him for another hour or so. During this part of our march, I checked the direction of the sun with my eye and realized that his geography had deserted him. We were once more circling. I called yet one more halt and we all consulted. Our tracker admitted that he was lost. Now, I had never been in a situation like this before and time was running out as the sun was no longer high above us (what we could see of it). We did not have food but a little water only. No light and naturally no sleeping facilities such as a blanket or something to lie on.

In a situation like that it is best to remain calm but this is not so easy. I could feel the vibes between the game scout and tracker becoming more tense than ever. The Indian hunter was jumpy and nervy. I had a suspicion that he was quietly blaming himself for coming on this hare-brained safari of mine. However, I did have a good knowledge of the size and shape of the forest and I knew that the longest section – i.e. one hundred miles stretched from north to south and that the narrowest section of fifty miles (all of which formed a rectangle) faced east and west. I doubt whether the game scout or our Indian knew this and I certainly did not think that our heroic tracker was aware of anything of the sort. Uneducated and illiterate he would probably have known a great deal about the area of forest close to his abode but nothing about size north or south etc.

We were discussing matters and I asked each one of them in turn in which direction he thought we should proceed. Low and behold – each gave directions that conflicted with the other. I looked at the murky forest, I could not decide on any direction. There was only one thing that I could think of to do so I took the spear from our tracker, (no I did not intend to skewer him) and stabbed the point into the ground making it stand as perpendicularly as possible. There was a dull light coming through the foliage high above us. A shadow was therefore cast by the spear on to the ground from the sun. With my finger I followed the shadow drawing a line along the sandy ground. After twenty minutes the shadow naturally had moved which now gave me a good idea where east, west, north and south were as it was past noon, so I pointed east, (which was the side into which we had entered), and said – "that way gentlemen". They did not understand my spear stabbing, shadow-drawing antics but as they had no idea whatsoever of the direction themselves, set off in the direction which I pointed out.

In reality, the tracker had done a good job as he had brought us back to a point not far from his *shamba* because, about one hour later, we exited almost bang-on to his abode. I was, however, perplexed that when we were so close to his home that he had lost his bearings and could not find his way out. He had not pointed east when I asked him in which direction we should go and nor had the others. I did not know; until the direction of movement of the shadow gave me the clue.

I slept very soundly that night in our tent. The following day I consulted our tracker and game scout and they informed me that there were plenty of buffalo in an area towards the Nile which was about twenty or thirty miles away. My Indian companion was keen to go after them but the other two had things to do – I think mainly to recover after our previous day of exercise.

We set off in the car travelling on a bush track for about fifteen miles when the track disappeared. We therefore pulled out our tent and prepared for the night. The following morning was spent trying to locate some local knowledge of the species and whereabouts of game. It was not easy as there appeared to be no human habitation, just bush which any hunter loves, but one had then to try and seek out the signs of animal tracks, dung, smells, etc. oneself. The Nile would have been about five miles ahead of us and we therefore thought that buffalo would not be difficult to find. The vegetation was mainly thick coarse matted grass about head-height with the odd tree here and there.

As there seemed to be no human signs and therefore no tracker to be engaged, we decided to remain in camp and set off the following day. The normal weather in this area of Uganda is humid. A temperature which hovers around 28C to 32C makes life very comfortable except when the hot sun is shining before, during and after midday.

Night time is rather cool so we built a fire and sat round this enjoying our corned beef, bread and butter, tinned peaches and some coffee but before this, I indulged in a beer or two. As I was abnormally fit I was able to consume beer at an uncommon rate with not a great deal of effect. Naturally a crate of beer was essential to keep my body in shape when on safari!

It is always a lovely part of the routine of safari life to settle in during the evening around a fire discussing the day's experiences over a drink or two and planning the action for the morrow. If animal life is in the area it is easily able to be identified by the sounds coming from the surrounding bush. The light from the fire attracts animals and unfortunately, insects. And of course, the ubiquitous mosquitoes.

The fascination of this part of a bush safari is well described by Bartle Bull in his superb book entitled *Safari – a Chronicle of Adventure* in his opening paragraph headed 'The Witchcraft of the Desert'. He writes:

> "The descent of the African night is never forgotten. There is nothing more complete than to rest by a fire on a canvas seat, with tobacco and a drink, as the sky grows blue dark and the stars sharpen with the clarity peculiar to Africa, until the rim of the firelight seems surrounded by a second, outer world alive with the night sounds of contrasting animals, and then to lie awake listening to the sounds of the bush, the low, panting grunt of lion, the sudden rush of hooves as zebra or antelope flee, the menacing cough of a leopard defending its kill from hyena."

The following day, a quick early breakfast. We then set off at daybreak. Buffalo seemed to be around. We spotted a herd on a hill on the other side of a valley. My trusty binoculars were used and the herd seemed to be about eighty to one hundred animals. The grass being so tall and thick meant that it was tough going but we kept to animal paths and were within about one hundred yards from them after three quarters of an hour. The wind was minimal but to see them in this tall grass was difficult in the extreme. My Indian friend (I think his name was Neil) was particularly keen to get his first buff. As we could not see more than fifteen feet in front of us I knew that our vigilance would have to be particularly acute. We crept closer to the herd and the grass thinned slightly so that we were able to see a little better but I did not want to get too close for fear of the lookout detecting us and the whole herd careering off as buffalo do. The wind was still holding off. It was blowing from the herd to us. Lucky. At about fifty yards, I could smell them distinctly but they seemed to be sensing our presence and when I looked through the binoculars for a decent spread of horns with a deep boss I could sense their unease. Two cows were looking directly towards our position.

At that stage I realized that there were a few which were not in the main herd and nearer to us. I indicated by signs whilst crouching low, to Neil, to decide whether he wanted to take one closer to us and handed him the binoculars. He seemed a little nervous but this was to be expected.

Things then happened fast. He handed me back the binoculars and had not yet made up his mind when a loud sound of hooves announced the presence (albeit galloping) of a buffalo in a thick clump of tall grass immediately to my right and in front of me about ten yards away. At this stage my safety catch was in the 'off' position so that I was ready to fire. I did not know in what direction the animal was travelling. All I had in front of me was the game path on which we were travelling and grass on either side, with the heavy grass clump on my right from which I expected the buffalo to charge. Rifle ready I waited standing still. Heart thumping. Nothing happened. Our buff had decided to join the herd and was speeding off to join his pals and did not confront us. Us did I say? I looked round and saw no-one where Neil was supposed to be. Walking back a few yards, maybe twenty, I saw him perched on the tree-trunk of a tree that had half fallen and which was at an angle which enabled him to run up the trunk and be about ten feet off the ground. So much for the back-up which I was hoping would be behind me if the buffalo had charged. I walked back to the spot where I had dropped the binoculars, in some disgust and surprise.

It would have made no sense to have him around as a back-up in the event of a charge from an elephant so I decided to part company and hunt for an elephant on my own. As mentioned earlier, I did enjoy hunting on my own unless I had one of my trusted 'old' hunting friends with me and which would have been fine but at that stage in East Africa most of my trusted hunting friends had left the country and I did not know anyone who would fit the bill in Uganda. I was therefore happy to say goodbye to this gentleman and not invite him to join me in my later quest for an elephant.

We travelled back to Kampala and it was at the time that Cynthia and I had arranged to vacate our house after our removers had packed up all our belongings and move into the Silver Springs Hotel for a further three weeks prior to our departure for the coast and eventually, after a further two weeks, to embark on the British India ship, *Karanja* at Mombasa. So whilst the family was in the hotel (Silver Springs), I was able to spend a further two or three weeks hunting for my final quarry.

11

The Last Hunt

I set off from Kampala for Masindi once more (loaded with food, beer and tent), reported to the District Commissioner, together with my valuable letter and informed him that I intended to hunt in the Karuma Falls area. He gave me permission immediately, after reading the letter from the Minister of Defence. I spent the night at the Masindi Hotel.

Full of enthusiasm I set off in the morning and travelled on the road from Masindi towards Gulu. After only a short distance of perhaps twenty five miles, I reached the Victoria Nile crossing and then shortly branched off west towards Karuma Falls. The road, once more, was just a bush track but as there had not been any heavy rains recently, was reasonably passable. The Peugeot 404 which I had used as a Land Rover, yes as a bush vehicle many times before, was particularly suitable for the job and once more never let me down although at times the going was very slow. I must have travelled a distance of perhaps twenty miles into the bush when I could see that the area appeared to be more interesting as villages were becoming progressively fewer and plenty of signs of elephant were evident. Just dung. It was also very beautiful open country with not many trees. As the track became increasingly less evident, I turned back to the last village and announced to a *duka* owner that I was looking for a tracker. Sitting chatting to him I found out that there were a number of elephant in the vicinity towards Karuma Falls but that no hunters had ventured into the area for many years. He had, in the meantime, sent out a runner

205

for a tracker and after about half an hour one arrived. He could speak enough Swahili to enable us to converse. I engaged him immediately as he seemed to be able to answer the normal questions one asked to ascertain if the applicant was an experienced tracker or just a chancer looking for a job, and there were plenty of them. Name – Daudi. This made me wonder how many trackers called themselves Daudi!

When travelling from this village westwards I was obliged to be very careful not to travel too far as the border of the Murchison Falls National Park was, in my calculations, about twenty five miles ahead of me. I did not want to be near it if I found a good pair of tusks.

I was most fortunate as I found that my new tracker was very handy in helping me set up camp after we had travelled about ten miles from the village. One can detect a 'bush boy' from a 'town swell' pretty soon. He was obviously one of the former. Whilst chatting to him near the fire that evening he questioned me regarding *my* ability to shoot. Had I shot many elephants before? No, not many. Well what had I shot if not elephant? I told him. Although he seemed satisfied with my credentials he said he would like me to shoot a target (tomorrow morning) just to get my eye in! I would imagine he had most likely had some hair-raising experiences with inexperienced hunting heroes before. Sitting round the fire in that glorious evening before the hunt, full of hopes I will never forget; me growing more and more impressed with my new tracker. I slept inside the car as it had fold-down seats enabling me to sleep well. Daudi was permitted to use my tent, which was a small one but which could accommodate two people. He had brought along a smelly blanket under which to sleep or to wrap around himself if the weather became cooler. He did not sport a spear.

After dawn a clear warm day was just appearing. I could see that the type of country I was to hunt in was absolutely beautiful – gently rolling plains with intermittent gullies, not deep, slight hills but most important of all, grass at knee height, with the tallest parts perhaps as high as the thigh – all very lush green. Just a very few thorn trees and low scrub. Some doum palms and groups of acacias.

Daudi sniffed the air like an eagerly impatient bloodhound. We engaged breakfast hastily after which he set up a target "for me to get my eye in". It was a piece of cardboard about six inches square and I managed to put three consecutive holes into it at twenty paces. I had passed his examination! I just hoped that we could get as close as twenty yards to any elephant I hoped to shoot.

When my great friend and elephant hunter Tony Marsh was hunting and he worked for the Agricultural Department in Mwingi in Kenya, he would send out one of his staff who would spend some days in the bush locating the herds and then reporting back the area in which he had espied a good pair of tusks, leaving someone to keep in contact with the herd. Tony would then proceed to the area and they would contact the 'herd-watcher' and hunt down the quarry.

I had no such luxury and Daudi and I would be tramping it out with binoculars and rifle in the days to come. As mentioned earlier, I was ultra fit and able to walk, slide, crawl, run, for up to ten hours at a fairly brisk pace without over-tiring myself. I don't know why but all my trackers whom I had worked with during my almost twenty years of hunting were short and wiry and never young. Wizened old campaigners, but not this one who was able to sprint faster than a hare, as I discovered later. I never saw or heard of a big tracker and although I did not realize it at the time, they were of course a dying breed. Over the years I developed an admiration and liking for the trackers and they became an integral part of the hunting; likeable companions who were almost like blood-brothers to the hunter as both hunters and trackers thrilled in the chase.

It was obvious that the area in which I was about to hunt would be nothing like as tough or as frustrating as the Budongo Forest for slipping and sliding up and down steep gullies, clambering over or ducking or crawling under fallen logs, thorns tearing at clothes and skin, with lack of vision ahead.

We set off on our first day and it became apparent that this was almost an untouched part of the country. There was a variety of game – antelope of all sorts including the unique Uganda Kob. It was no more than a few hours when Daudi was on to the scent of elephant, or should I say – on to the tracks and smells of elephant. Uganda is a country which is hot, damp underfoot and humid. This means that footprints are comparatively easy to pick out and follow. Daudi became absorbed in the sizes of footmark, number of footmarks and was carefully studying the niceties of dung appearance, freshness, smell and texture, pointing out to me what he detected the pachyderms had been eating. This latter point is most important because if one knows what vegetation the animals have been eating, it gives one a clue as to the whereabouts of his meal times such as doum palms, (borassus aethiopium) and sometimes called fan palms which have yellow fleshy fruits and which elephant love and consider a great delicacy. When ripe, the fruit contains alcohol and the elephants consume this, dozing happily and a little 'tipsy' under the shade of these very large palms.

Some hunters I knew were of the opinion that the hunter should only look ahead and ignore the work of the tracker but I did not agree with this entirely as I found it so interesting to observe what he was doing to enable us to find our quarry. Naturally, when nearing the prey, matters changed.

It is now 2006 as I write this and I cannot, for the life of me, remember how many days it took to locate a sizeable pair of tusks but I think it was probably four or five.

During those four or five days, we walked a considerable number of miles, viewed up to fifty elephant per day and found that stalking them was not all that difficult except for one unusual hindrance which I had not encountered before and which I had never heard of previously. At times, some of the elephant herds had formed a partnership with wild pigs, yes wild pigs. They would graze on the outside of the herd and become alarmed at our approach long before the elephant, then scamper off, giving the jumbos some sort of warning of our presence. This happened three or four times before it made us doubly cautious as we had to take into account wind direction, location of pigs, whether north, south east or west, if the ten or so pigs were present. The elephants would then take off and that would be the end of our stalking efforts. Most frustrating, but fortunately not all herds had these partnerships and our stalking techniques were comparatively successful most times. I was becoming impatient at having viewed about two or three hundred elephant and not one sizeable pair of tusks. The fact that the country in which we were hunting was so beautiful and comfortable to walk in with so much other game as well, compensated to some degree for my frustration. What also really made it so unusual was the total lack of human habitation – what bliss! It rained at times but this did not hinder us much as the weather was warm and our clothes dried quickly after a downpour.

It was mid-morning on the fourth or fifth day of our safari when I spotted, with my naked eye, the glint in the sunlight of a pair of tusks. The herd was approximately three quarters of a mile away on the rise of a slight slope of land ahead of us. There were about thirty to forty in the herd. It is a most interesting sight to see a pair of good tusks glinting in the sun, some distance away. After looking at so many 'pegs' for day after day, the sight of this ivory started the adrenalin pumping and I looked through the binoculars for confirmation. Yes, the tusks were thick and undamaged, not very long but the heavy thickness made up for this.

I searched the low scrub and knee-high grass for wild pigs – none to be seen. Wind, very slight and from a direction that would necessitate our moving to our right for about a quarter of a mile before stalking. The grass being only knee-height with not much scrub and no trees, it was obvious that a long, low crouching stance, then crawling on stomach was to be our approach. I felt that I needed Daudi as he could test wind continually, leaving me to decide how to approach as I wished when nearing the herd. I asked if he would like to accompany me and he was excited and eager. From then on it was go, go, go – crouching, crawling and keeping as straight a line as possible with him directly behind me. This is unquestionably necessary as the poor sight of an elephant will pick up a sideways movement more easily than one that is keeping a straight line towards it. As we crept closer over a period of about one hour, I was relieved to see that the herd was resting and not feeding. There were no trees in sight and there seemed to be no wild pigs about. I used the binoculars at intervals to confirm this. It is also important to make sure that the binoculars are used at an angle that will not reflect the sun towards the eyes of the herd from the lenses. My trusty tracker kept sucking his index finger and holding it up to test wind direction. Occasionally he picked up sand and watched it fall.

As we approached, and at about fifty or sixty yards, I could not see my quarry clearly as the old bull had two very attentive *askaris*, (minders) one on each side looking after him. This was frustrating but I had to be patient and wait until they moved, when I was within shooting range and which I intended to be about thirty yards or closer.

It was now a case of continuous belly-crawling as silently as possible. And never to fiddle with anything metallic on the rifle as the sound of any metallic click would have been picked up by the herd and set them careering off. Fortunately my weapon had a safety-catch that was absolutely silent. This enabled me to keep it in the 'on' position until the very last moment.

All went well and I eventually reached what I considered to be as close as possible. Any closer and I feared the herd would have detected us. At this point we were twenty-seven paces away, (I measured it after all the dust had settled) and the two *askaris* seemed to be protecting the old bull admirably – not letting me see any part of his head.

I had chosen once more to go for a brain shot. Karamoja Bell had been so successful in his hunting career with this method that I intended to emulate his practice as near as possible. According to the description in his book, aim at a point in the head where, if one drew an imaginary line from eye to ear hole, bisected it; then raised the intended point of entry two inches up on the bi-section, entry to the brain would take place provided that one was at right angles to the head and provided that one was not too close; so that the trajectory would be comparatively parallel to the ground and not pointing in an upward incline.

I had slowly raised myself into a sitting position in order to have a steadier aim with elbows on knees. I must say that as I frustratingly sat waiting for a clear view of the head as described above, my heart was thumping terribly, banging against my ribcage alarmingly. It seemed like a lifetime that I was sitting rooted to the ground waiting for that one *askari*, on my side of the bull to move away. There were cows to my left and right closer to us than the bull. Cows are normally very much more on the alert than bulls and I had to keep a wary eye on them. It could not have been more than, perhaps three or four minutes but it seemed like an absolute age. The wind was non-existent, behaving nicely. Finally the bull inched forward and then stopped. The attendant *askari* was a trifle slow in moving forward and this, at last, gave me a clear view of the old bull's head.

I aimed and squeezed the trigger.

When a .375 Magnum rifle is fired the explosion and kick are always exciting; especially so when the hunter feels he has found his mark. A dull thud is normally heard almost immediately after the explosion.

The old bull gave an ever-so-slight shudder, visible for a few split seconds and then the great beast started to sway very gently on his legs, then, in almost slow motion, slid backwards into a sitting position as the back legs collapsed. Immediately from that sitting position this huge animal then rolled over away from me on to its side, legs protruding towards me.

I sat there totally mesmerized at the enormity of the scene before me and the rest of the herd was also numbed into a very short period of paralysis. Not for long – only a very few seconds. Then sheer pandemonium broke out. The cows trumpeted and started milling around with trunks up and ears extended, presumably looking, listening and sniffing to find out where their enemy was located. It did not take them long; the riposte was swift and the whole herd then started stampeding straight towards us. *"Kimbiya bwana"* shouted my tracker and we then scrambled to our feet and started a high-speed sprint away from the herd. Fortunately for the two of us, the ground was flat and the grass only knee-height on a slight downward slope and this, plus the adrenalin pumping through our anatomies enabled us to keep up a pretty brisk pace.

Whoever it was, or probably whoever they were who estimated or gave learned opinion on whether man could outrun or outpace an elephant were entirely wrong when they pontificated that elephant was faster than man. Not so.

For the first hundred yards or so we did gain on them. When one runs for one's life, perhaps the adrenalin rush spurs the body into heights of speed which would not normally be attained on the athletics track.

As we ran I would estimate that they were approximately twenty to thirty yards behind us but what alarmed me was that they seemed to be after us.

Now, when an elephant runs, the skin in the 'armpits' or 'legpits' above the front legs and the same for the rear legs, makes a sound like very rough leather being rubbed together and this, when there are about thirty elephant running is quite pronounced and audible as there is no sound from the feet at all. This scrape-scrape is a sound that I would guess not many people have heard except some hardened old professional hunters. I will never forget it. This eerie sound was creeping closer and closer.

After the initial sixty or seventy yards, or maybe one hundred (I did not count), our pace was starting to slacken due to exhaustion and the herd was gaining on us. I looked around and at this stage was looking upwards at elephants which were definitely beginning to get too close, maybe fifteen to twenty yards. The thought entered my mind that if I stopped and fired over their heads, it would perhaps turn them but then I realized that if they did not, I would be in serious trouble as I could only fire two more shots in quick succession at a herd of thirty beasts who seemed to be bent on running down their enemy. The hunters had become the hunted.

There was only one thing left to do and so I called to Daudi to follow me and swung off at a tangent to my left and at right angles. Mercifully the herd swept straight on and on and on. I looked at the great retreating animals in awe and astonishment as they gradually disappeared from sight, and the haunting scrape-scrape sound receded into the distance with them.

We had both sunk down into a sitting position with lungs at bursting point and a feeling of relief overtaking us entirely.

Gradually, the realization that I had accomplished my goal started to sink in through the feeling of relief of still being in one piece.

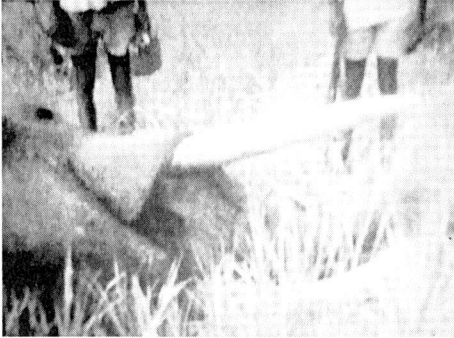
A good pair of tusks

Whilst recovering with pulses racing, still panting and perspiring from a close shave with death, my thoughts turned to Tony Marsh and his cautionary advice to me – "the downing of the elephant which has the big tusks is a lot easier than dealing with the attendant cows who can then do all sorts of unexpected things to get at the hunter".

My thoughts also turned to my very good friend Arthur Weston in Dar es Salaam who had been caught by the cows and trampled to death after downing his quarry.

However, elation soon took over but I had to ask Daudi one very important question. Did that herd intend to run us down and then deal with us or were they just stampeding? His opinion was that had they been bent on wreaking revenge on us they would have followed when we turned left and easily caught and dealt with us. Well, I will never know, it remains an unanswered question.

We hastened back to the initial point of action to find my elephant lying prone on his side, still in the same position where he fell. I did the precautionary final shot into the brain and then inspected the tusks which were quite short but rather nice and thick. It was obvious that the quality was good and completely undamaged. There was not a happier hunter in this world at that time, than myself. Daudi seemed to have forgotten the narrow escape we had had. He was generous with his praise.

I rushed back to the car which must have been three or four miles away to get the cine camera. It was now nearing evening and the sky was turning dark which meant rain. On the way back a downpour enveloped me but this did not worry me in the least as I felt so elated. The sky cleared and allowed a small amount of camera work to be carried out. I then did a much more intense scrutiny of my tusks etc and the enormity of the whole episode started to sink in.

It soon became dark so we made our way back to camp near the car, wet clothes clinging to my skin but I hardly noticed it as I was so exhilarated at the outcome of the whole event. The beer therefore tasted like Moet et Chandon and I indulged copiously as did Daudi whose capacity for bottled *mzungu* beer (*pombe)* seemed inexhaustible.

Author sitting on trophy

Up early the next morning and after a slice of bread and a cup of coffee, set off and arrived at the previous day's scene of action with axe and *panga*. (East African bush knife). Daudi scoffed at these cutting tools and assured me that we would soon have company and that all forms of bush scalpels would be provided by the visiting human armada that he expected. I asked how knowledge of our previous day's action would be conveyed to the locals and he pointed to the sky and high above us where vultures were circling. "Yes" he said, "they would soon be here as our presence and intentions would have been spread throughout the village and scouts would be waiting for signs and would appear, then send messages of my success back to the village. Within a couple of hours two scouts turned up and one hastily set off at a slow sprint back to the village with the news.

Early afternoon and the horde of meat-eaters started to arrive. Action started immediately and I was happy and curious to see them get to work. They had brought more than a dozen spear heads which were to be used as knives, a special knife sharpening stone, *kerais* (wide bowls) and a scrappy piece of canvas about fifteen feet long and six feet wide, firewood and gourds of native beer, some water, *pangas*. This impressive array of slicing utensils etc was soon set in action and the canvas propped up to make a barrier against the sun for the knife-sharpener and the fire so that cooks could prepare barbecued elephant unlimited.

There must have been about twenty-five of them and they were very happy to receive all this meat – free. I picked two young braves whom I thought would be able to cope with the removal of the tusks. Two strong-looking lads.

Action commenced and an incision was made in the stomach which, now that the animal was lying on its side, was round and rising to about five feet in height. They opened it up and spread it apart so that they could burrow in and then eventually walk inside.

The knives (spearheads) were being sharpened frequently while the sharpener was kept busy doing nothing else as blades had to be razor-sharp to enable those doing the butchering to cut through, first of all, the skin and then intestines and latterly the edible meat. The perspiring 'butchers' would frequently take a choice piece of meat to the fire after handing in knives to the sitting sharpener to hone for further action; and cook over the fire - but it all looked desperately underdone to me. They all seemed to do the same and enjoyed eating with great gusto. Some women were tending the fire and sometimes they would do the cooking. A great aroma of cooking elephant meat arose from the two fires and all those workers were a very very happy lot. Those with the *kerais* approached the action area and placed them on the ground behind those grappling with the cutting from the body, of the meat. After *kerais* were filled and placed on the head, the bearer would then start on the long journey back to the village where he, (or she) would have sufficient meat for a feast for the whole family and more left over for cooking and providing for their needs for the next week. Some pieces would be smoked and therefore edible for a few weeks hence.

The knife sharpener worked non-stop for hour after hour.

By sunset, only a third of the vast amount of meat had been removed and all then relaxed and filled their bellies with meat and drank the *pombe* they had brought with them. I moved off back to my camp which was now only about half-a-mile away. During the day I had gone back to the car, and with the help of one of the 'workers' whom I had requisitioned, struck camp and driven to near the scene of action.

Cooking was still taking place and serious meat-eating carried on unabated. I did not believe that they could eat any more but I was wrong – their capacity seemed never-ending. I indulged in a small steak (which I cooked) and found it to be rather different in taste to the normal domestic or venison steaks which we are accustomed to.

However, my main task was the supervision of the removal of the tusks. Approximately one third of the tusk lies buried in extremely tough gristly matter and *pangas* and knives seem to make only a little progress at a time. Furthermore, my valiant pair of tusk surgeons were unable to understand much Swahili and were more interested in the steaks being brought to them than the delicate task of cutting into this very tough matter around the tusks without damaging them. It required all my very close guidance and they seemed to think that my fastidious attention was unnecessary. When one of them was handed a gourd of *pombe*, I immediately dispensed with his services and took on a fresh operator which required even more of my attention than previously. It took hours and hours but eventually we were able to ease one tusk from left to right and forwards and backwards. Tugging and manoeuvring round eventually freed the first one and then the next. There was only one small axe-chip in one of them.

This was not the end of the operation.

The nerve inside an elephant tusk is a round and tapering shape which culminates in a point some three and a half feet into the tusk. The beginning of the nerve protrudes out of the base about six to eight inches. My two heroes did not know how to cope with the removal of this tough jelly-like-substance. Daudi did. He took one of the 'knives' and pierced it at right angles through the protruding base until the point had gone right through to the other side. He then gave the knife a hard twist and pull. The whole nerve slithered out in one long piece, a tapering piece of grey opaque tough jelly. The onlookers and Daudi looked in horror at it and I asked if it was edible and this drew gasps of disgust from all of them. None would touch it and drew back in revulsion. I bent down and stroked it; it was quite smooth and slightly slimy. I agreed – not edible.

The next task, and which was just as difficult as the tusks was the dislodgment of the feet. A number of arduous hours then ensued. These, of course, are removed and hollowed out then later handed over to a taxidermist to make side-tables.

One last consideration; the hairs which are nice and easy to sever and these make rather neat, if masculine, bracelets if and when one can find the clever *fundis* who can tie the especial knots required to make an expanding and contracting bracelet. I was very lucky to find one much later, sitting cross-legged in a street in Mombasa, busy doing just that. A wizened old Arab who was happy to tie my couple of dozen hairs into bracelets, for a fee.

After many farewell *salaams* from these very likeable and primitive villagers and my tracker, I loaded tusks, feet, etc into my trusty Peugeot station-wagon and proceeded to the District Commissioner in Masindi to have the tusks weighed, recorded and stamped with a number. I also sent a telegram to Cynthia advising that my mission had been accomplished.

The weight - fifty-eight pounds and fifty-nine pounds respectively. Almost symmetrical in shape, very good quality; and weights unusually similar. The weights – well, nothing to be shouted about but, in my eyes, a handsome trophy. The experience – an indelible print on my nostalgia-filled memory.

Cynthia, Jimmy and tusks circa 1975

12

Final thoughts

Having spent nigh-on twenty years in East Africa I look back on it as a marvellous period in my life. The greatest day I had was the day of my marriage. The births of our four children in East Africa were enjoyable highlights. Graham and John were born in the European hospital in Dar es Salaam, Julia in the Princess Elizabeth Hospital in Nairobi and Michael in Mulago Hospital in Kampala. True East Africans by birth.

The old colonial life was not a period of relaxing pleasure. We in commercial life worked hard and enjoyed our leisure pursuits. Not to say that government servants did not work hard; they were, almost-to-a-man dedicated civil servants who spent their lives and a considerable amount of time in very primitive malaria-infested conditions, developing the country and bettering the life of the indigenous population. This is contrary to what a very large proportion of people, who are totally ignorant of the part played by the expatriate communities in colonial times think, and spread in the media today.

We had our lives turned topsy-turvy at times, such as the overthrow of the Kabaka (King) of Buganda, the mutiny of the army in Tanganyika, then the mutiny of the army in Kenya. The latter two mutinies were quelled with ease and very rapidly by the intervention of the British Army at the request of the newly-fledged incoming indigenous governments.

We lived and worked in malaria-infested conditions. Dysentery was a fairly commonplace occurrence and mango-fly eggs inhabited our clothes when left on the laundry line too long and then entered our skin. Another hazard but not so frequent was tick-fever. Bilharzia existed in all the rivers and lakes and especially the still water or edges of the water near the banks. If one swam in these waters the danger would be that the bilharzias parasite would enter the pores of the skin and the hapless host would suffer immensely with both the disease and the old-fashioned methods of cure – long syringe- needles into the stomach. I was unlucky enough to contract all these diseases with the exception of bilharzia.

Today, hunting is taboo. Thoughts propounded in many parts of the world and the ridiculous postulations of such organizations as the Green Party and animal rights campaigners here in the UK I find to be totally absurd. Yes, today, the wildlife must be preserved at all costs. I do agree with the great researcher Bartle Bull who wrote in *Safari* that banning all hunting in East Africa and Kenya in particular, has exacerbated the problem. Why? Because the presence of controlled hunting kept the hunters in the domains of the wild animals. All hunters of repute did value and indeed cherish the wild animals and their domains and were passionate in their loathing of these hideous poachers.

Due to the vacuum caused by the absence of hunters, banning of hunting became a siren to the poachers to go ahead in such numbers that the newly independent governments were unable to provide the finance for a sufficiently large force of anti-poaching *askaris* to cope with the problem.

We hunted what one could call selectively. To expand – let me say that we shot for the pot, for the skin or for a trophy but never for reward financially. Yes, the old 'white hunters' did hunt for financial gain from shooting and selling ivory; it was their means of living. This was in the early part of the twentieth century when game was so prolific that the number of animals shot made only a miniscule difference to the overall total population.

It was civilization and human population explosion that decided the fate of the grand old days when game outnumbered human population. As David Attenborough has recently (2007) explained, humans are now multiplying on this planet faster than rats.

Regarding my hunting, I make no apologies whatsoever for the great times I and many others enjoyed 'in the bush'. In previous chapters I have expounded on the absolute thrill of my experiences, and the sheer beauty of unspoiled plains with herds of animals. Of the incomparable magnificence of sylvan views which abound in East Africa.

The simple joys of the smell of canvas when entering one's tent after a day's hunting. The thought that your tent is a refuge (home) from the weather and is easily raised and lowered and transported to anywhere of one's choice in beautiful surroundings. The clear air with a delicate aroma of wild flowers. The happy, cheerful camp boys who are anticipating the gorging of barbequed venison. A gorgeous multicoloured sunset to quietly behold. The gentle sound of the wild birds, the aroma of a wood fire. Sitting round it in the evenings and either enthusing about the day's events or planning for the following day. The aroma of cooking. These are some of the unparalleled classic joys of life in the bush. I quote once more from Bartle Bull's book *Safari*:

> "For many, then and now, President Roosevelt epitomized the apparent Jekyll and Hyde dilemma of the hunter-conservationist. In Europe, Africa and America, the most effective conservationists have often been the most dedicated hunters. It is difficult for non-shooters to accept this reality. They will not believe that serious hunters truly love and protect the creatures they kill. In fact, most hunters and the conservationists share a love of nature. Critics of hunting often assume that the conservation effort of hunters are merely self-serving, limited to prolonging their own depredations. This is an error both as to physical results and attitude. More interesting, it fails to perceive the inspiration of hunting. The protection of an animal or an acre also preserves the creatures that interrelate with it, including people. Hunters and fishermen everywhere, like Theodore Roosevelt and Frederik Selous, actively supported conservation and environmental programmes from which they would never personally benefit".

As I conclude writing today, in 2009, Zambia allows hunting under strict rules controlled by their government and this brings in a welcome amount of financial assistance to a cash-strapped country. We all hope that the forward-thinking authorities of Zambia will build up the wild life population there and that this proves to be a lesson to those countries which have not followed suit and should do so.

London, May 2009

Glossary

askari	guard, minder or policeman
aya	child minder
baobab	indigenous thick-trunked tree
biltong	smoked and dried meat
bush (gone bush)	rejecting civilisation
bwana	sir
debbi	four gallon tin
duka	shop
duka wallah	shop owner
fundi	teacher or expert
gharry	car
godown	warehouse
kanzu	long, white robe with no pockets
kerai	shallow tin basin
kikuyu	Kenya tribe
kimbiya bwana	run sir
kongoni	hartebeest (antelope)
kumi	ten
lateen rigged	single, triangular dhow sail
luo	Kenya tribe
mabati	corrugated iron sheet
madafu	immature coconut

makuti	palm leaves (used for roofing)
mara moja	immediately
memsahab	lady of the house
mpishi	cook
mzee	old
mzungu	white man
ngalawa	canoe with two outriggers and sail
ngombe	cow or ox
panga	East African bush knife
pombe	liquor
rondavel	round thatched room
Rufiji	name of a river
safi	clean or pure
salaams	greetings, introductory or farewell
serikali	police
shamba	garden, field or farm
shillingi	shillings
toto	young boy
uhuru	freedom (independence)
wazungu	white man

2015

My Cynthia died in 2011. A wonderful lady and a devout Christian all her life. I am devastated and I have found that time is no healer. My monumental grieving does not abate.

JT